OLYMPIA 420
·THE QUEST FOR PEACE·

J.B. DATH

WITH ILLUSTRATIONS BY
JENNIFER BARRETTE

HERZOG HOUSE PUBLISHING

Herzog House Publishing
Permissions Department
www.herzoghouse.com

Book Design by Jennifer Barrette and Genie Gold

Dath, J.B.
Olympia 420: *The Quest for Peace*: a novel / J.B. Dath

Summary:
A young athlete revives the recently ignored Olympic Games in the hope that the
Olympic Truce will save Athens' democracy from destruction by aggressive Sparta and
bring lasting peace to war-torn ancient Greece.

[1. Historical — Fiction. 2. Fantasy — Fiction. 3. Ancient Greece — Fiction.
4. War — Fiction. 5. Olympic Games — Fiction.] I. Title

Library of Congress Control Number 2005920434

ISBN 0-9763086-0-6

Printed in the United States of America
First American Edition: March 2005

10 9 8 7 6 5 4 3 2 1

To Jenn

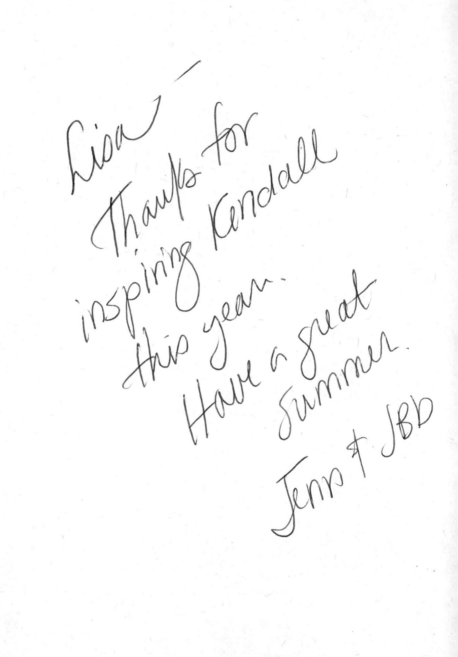

Lisa —
Thanks for
inspiring Kendall
this year.
Have a great
summer.

Jenn & JBB

TABLE OF CONTENTS

Prologue 1

1. Champion of Elis 5

2. Blood-Red and Shining Bronze 13

3. The Dream Lives 33

4. Wolves 51

5. Athens 71

6. Amazons 91

7. Coming into Place 107

8. Let the Games Begin 125

9. The Hot Night After 141

10. Leather in the Face 151

11. The Plot Thickens 169

12. The Chariot Race 177

13. Besieged and Battered 189

14. A Pointed End 203

15. Pankration 223

16. All Hail 239

CAST OF CHARACTERS

AENEAS	Orion's younger cousin
ALCIBIADES	Ambitious nephew of Pericles
ANTIOPE	Scar-faced Amazon queen
ARCHIDAMUS	Younger Spartan king
ARGIVE	Speedy Champion of Argos
ARIA	Orion's inspiring love interest
BRASIDAS	Rugged Spartan general
CADMUS	Orion's puny best friend
CLEON	Elderly Speaker of the Athenian Council
DEMOSTHENES	Valiant Athenian general and Champion of Athens
EURIPEDES	Suspicious Athenian guard captain
HERAK	Nordic-blooded Champion of Thebes
HERODOTUS	Father of History
HIPPOCRATES	Father of Medicine
HIPPONAX	Orion's friend and opponent
HIPPOLYTA	Penthesilea's sultry Amazon rival
IBYCUS	Flamboyant Elean announcer
KONON	Quarry worker and Champion of Corinth
LYCURGUS	Older Spartan king
MARATHON	Dashing Athenian captain
MEMNON	African mercenary hired as Champion of Mantinea
MEDEA	Aria's assertive sister
NESTOR	Defiant Helot (serf to Spartans)
NICIAS	Cautious Athenian general
ORION	Champion of Elis
PENTHESILEA	Catlike Champion of the Amazons
PERICLES	Athenian political leader (deceased)
PYTHEAS	Aria's merchant father
SOCRATES	Athenian philosopher and teacher
SOLORCHUS	Chief Hellanodike (Olympic administrator)
TERPANDER	Spartan army captain

PROLOGUE

In 2004, in Athens, a construction worker shoveled away the last earth from a four-inch section of ancient pottery. Immediately, the worker called to his companions, and together, breaths shallow with reverent excitement, they carefully exhumed the artifact.

Remarkably, the cylindrical clay jar was intact, a classic example of its city's ancient Golden Age. A foot tall and ten inches in circumference, the jar's sides (decorated with reddish-brown figures set against a black background) depicted a slender young athlete besting an older, more robust opponent at pankration—the terrible combat sport in which everything was permitted except gouging the eyes and biting. But most intriguing of all, the round stopper at the narrow top of the spectacular artifact had been fired shut; by shaking, it was clear that something not very heavy, perhaps weighing a pound, had been stuffed inside the pot.

The worker who made the discovery, accompanied by his foreman—both sweaty and covered in silt—hurried the find to the nearby archeological museum. Soon the curator, with his foremost

colleagues and the two laborers all huddled excitedly around, sat inside his office at his desk, with the artifact in his hands. The curator carefully twisted the stopper loose, placed it on the desktop, and looked into the jar as light flooded its interior for the first time in over twenty-four hundred years. His eyes got bigger. Then he reached his hand inside to extract a papyrus scroll: as tall as the container, tightly wrapped, and fastened in the middle with a piece of brown string. The curator untied the string and unfurled the parchment to reveal a phenomenon more stunning than the container it came in—a previously unknown record of the bitter conflict that engulfed the Greek world in intermittent fighting for twenty-seven years, 431 BC to 404 BC, leaving it spent and in tatters.

❧

Modern man already knows of other accounts of the Peloponnesian War; but those other accounts do not provide a complete picture. The newly discovered description fills gaps in our information, adding exciting details to previously known events and revealing whole new happenings that until now had remained lost in time. And it even introduces us to an important but previously unheard-of historical personality, Orion of Elis. He was not a general or a politician but a young man who came from quite average circumstances. Yet, when he was called by the chaotic tide of events, he answered with unexpected resourcefulness and valor, risking all and passing through great peril to inspire almost everyone with the hope of lasting peace.

This new understanding of the Peloponnesian War could not have come at a more appropriate time; in many ways the dynamics of that conflict mirror those faced by the world today. Long-standing tensions erupting into hostility between two fundamentally opposed ways of life. Both sides afraid of destruction by the other, as they struggle to decide the future shape of the world.

Because this new, hopeful account of the most bitter of ancient Greek conflicts serves as such a strong analogy for present-day circumstances, many believe that these past happenings can teach us something we can use to better understand the deep divides of our era. And perhaps these past happenings can even inspire us to resolve our present conflicts. Therefore, I have translated their telling for modern audiences, taking great care to observe the tradition of the greatest chroniclers of events of all eras, including the ancient Greeks, by making the material easily understandable and enjoyable to the people of my own time while preserving as much of the source material as possible. In these regards, I hope I have served both you and the original author well.

His name is Dramacles, nephew of Herodotus, the man considered by our generation as the Father of History because he was the first writer to conduct an ordered investigation of facts. However, Herodotus also has been called the Father of Lies, due to his reputation for adding fantastical details to embellish his accounts. And it is impossible to know which of his famous uncle's tendencies Dramacles embraced more closely.

Chapter One

CHAMPION OF ELIS

I am Dramacles of Athens, nephew of the great historian Herodotus of Halicarnassus, and this is my investigation. I have set it forward in these pages to record the great and vile deeds of men, to show why whole peoples fought each other and the consequences of their struggles, and to preserve these universal human truths for succeeding generations.

The city of Elis was located on a plain at the west of the Peloponnesian Peninsula. Olympia, the sports complex where the great Olympic Games always had been held, was just a few miles from it and not, though named in honor of the home of Zeus, proximate to Mount Olympus, hundreds of miles away, in the northeastern region of Greece known as Thessaly.

Since no one actually lived at Olympia, the honor of acting as hosts of the Olympic Games always had fallen to the Eleans. Their reputation for absolute fairness in doing so (widely cemented through the entire ancient world) assured them of that role, which they steadfastly fulfilled under the command of the Hellanodikes,

the ten men in purple royal robes who possessed absolute authority over administering all aspects of the grand event.

In the spring of every fourth year, for over three hundred years,
the Hellanodikes had dispatched heralds to travel throughout
Greece to announce the Olympic Truce and the upcoming competition to be held in August. Always, wars (if there were any) stopped
temporarily so that everyone could attend. But then, eleven years
ago, the year after the games were last held, a bitter struggle began
beyond the steep mountains to the east of Elis. And the war continued for several years until the spring of the year when the
Olympic Games were to have been next celebrated. At that time, as
they always had done, the Hellanodikes of Elis dispatched the
heralds. But, instead of agreeing to observe the long-held custom
of peace, some of the warring cities refused the truce on that
occasion. And they did so again, four years later, as the conflict
raged on.

With no truce agreed, both times the Olympic Games did not
take place. And so the Hellanodikes, three years ago, to keep the
spirit of athletic competition alive, started the local Elean Games,
to be held at the end of every summer among the residents of their
city.

At the center of life in Elis was the Agora, the busy market to
which people came daily to fill their basic needs for goods, food,
and conversation. Around the Agora's rectangular perimeter, permanent shops, with walls made of mud bricks, sat under colonnades covered by red clay-tile roofs. Between the perimeter shops,
at the center of the marketplace, was an open-air area with a dirt

floor. There, merchants of every kind usually placed their commodities on tables underneath their stalls, which generally consisted of a square roof of brightly colored cloth that was supported by a tall wooden pole at each corner.

But on this last day of the rain-drenched Third Elean Games, though by now the drops had stopped coming down, the center of the Agora looked quite different. The stalls all had been cleared away, replaced by a roped wrestling ring with four wooden corner posts. On the muddy ground around the ring stood a crowd of spectators, packed shoulder-to-shoulder outside the ropes, all the way back to underneath the colonnades. And the spectators, dressed in their finest tunics, together formed one excited, surging sea of color—reds, yellows, greens, blues, whites, and browns.

Thirty-year-old Ibycus (the tall, painfully slim announcer with brown, shoulder-length hair and a flair for high drama) stood in his blue linen tunic at the center of the ring's muddy floor. He was addressing the crowd as only a showman of his flamboyance could—gestures, body gyrations, and voice fluctuations. "The winner of this contest becomes the athletic champion of all Elis; and so, without further delay, it is my pleasure to introduce the two men who compete for that honor."

The crowd cheered, filling the Agora with sound, and Ibycus waited for it to stop. "In this corner we have the thirty-five-year-old challenger, Hipponax," he continued, pointing at the giant with the massive barrel chest. Big-boned Hipponax stood six-foot-four, a yard wide, and he weighed 280 pounds, not a muscle visible under his fat. His massive head was covered by bushy, dark, curly hair. He had a big, chubby face; a short beard of similar wiry hair; a medium-sized, square nose; and small, dark, crazy eyes.

Now the wild giant stepped out into the middle of the ring and bent over. He thrust his hands down towards the ground and scooped up two handfuls of thick, dark mud, which he smeared across his arms and face. Then he stood up straight again and rumbled a menacing growl at his opponent. "Grrr!"

Twenty-one-year-old Orion, standing calmly in the opposite corner, could not have made a more striking contrast. He had the kind of body they modeled statues after, six-foot-one, 210 sleek pounds of perfectly proportioned muscle. And he was handsome— straight, medium-length, sandy-blonde hair; strong, balanced features; just the right fullness to his lips; and large, curious yet knowing, doe-like, brown eyes.

"Orion, look on the bright side; at least he doesn't have any teeth left," said Cadmus, Orion's best friend, standing right outside his corner. The same age as Orion, Cadmus was far less physically imposing, five-foot-four, 140 skinny pounds. And he was no beauty. He had lots of soft, wispy, medium-length, light-brownish hair. His eyes and features were similar to Orion's, yet they did not have the same sharpness or strength.

"And in this corner," Ibycus continued to the crowd, "I present the never-defeated two-time defending champion—the young, the handsome, the noble, Orion!"

Again the crowd cheered as Orion walked towards the center of the ring. Then he arrived, and the onlookers silenced, nervously anticipating the start of the match. Hipponax was dangerous. His aggressive style of wrestling had crushed all previous opponents at these games.

"Keep it clean," warned Ibycus, looking right at Hipponax as he retreated to the ropes. Then he turned and ducked under the top cord to exit the ring, leaving the two athletes circling each other, ready to pounce.

"Now you're mine," Hipponax snarled, right before he suddenly lurched forward, trying to catch Orion by surprise. Orion quickly stepped back and away. Hipponax missed, lost balance, teetered for a moment as he tried to regain it, and then his feet slipped out from underneath his massive weight, and he fell face-first into the splattering muck.

Orion, pressing his advantage, immediately moved over Hipponax and sat down hard on his back, with his two feet planted, one on each side, solid on the ground. Then he placed both his hands under the wild man's chin and tugged it firmly up and back. Hipponax, unable to see through the slop coating his eyes and the rest of his face, tried to roll first to one side and then to the next, so that he could topple the young champion underneath him. But no matter which direction he tried to turn, Orion pulled his head the other way, forcing him back to where they started.

"Orion has caught himself a pig," Cadmus called to the other spectators. Already amused at seeing the previously untamed giant rolling around in the mud, now they openly laughed.

This only enraged Hipponax more as he struggled, without success, to pry Orion's hands away from his chin. "Grrr."

"Do you surrender?" asked Orion.

"Never," Hipponax barked. Then he tried again to spin Orion off and under him. But Orion was not about to give up his advantage. This time he applied even more force.

Hipponax realized he could not escape. "Okay. I give up. I give up!"

Orion released his hold and jumped off the giant's back, quicker than he had gotten on. "How's the neck?"

"It's a little stiff, but I'll be alright," answered Hipponax, wiping his eyes clean as Orion helped him up.

"No hard feelings," said Orion, sticking his hand out to shake.

"Of course not, Orion," replied Hipponax, grasping it. "But don't think I won't try just as hard to get you next time." The two men had nothing but respect for each other. They were friends outside the ring, bonded by their common love of sport. But it was that same love that made them such fierce rivals inside the ropes. Each man refused to dishonor the true spirit of athletic competition by performing at anything less than his absolute best within the confines of the rules, even if that meant using a little intimidation or inflicting pain.

"I expect nothing else," said Orion, smiling as they released the handshake. Meanwhile, Solorchus, the Chief Hellanodike (a fifty-year-old, fat, smirking man with ruffled, brown hair and beard) strutted pompously into the ring, holding an olive wreath. Then he walked over to the two athletes and placed the garland on Orion's head to crown him champion. The olive garland was the only prize for winning the Elean Games, just as it had been at the Olympic Games. The honor of becoming champion was more than enough reward. No other was necessary to any of the athletes.

Now the spectators could not contain themselves any longer, and they stormed inside the ropes to congratulate the gracious winner, pushing aside everyone else. Hipponax willingly eased out of the ring, eager to let Orion have his due. But Solorchus, remaining next to Orion, trying to claim the young victor's glory, arrogantly refused to cede even a step to the crowd (which had no interest in him), and he accidentally ended up on the ground with thick, dark slop all over his royal clothes.

Chapter Two

BLOOD-RED AND SHINING BRONZE

Several centuries before the events recounted here, the Greek world emerged from the Dark Age in its current form—a collection of hundreds of city-states on the mainland and spread across the waters to the shores of the Mediterranean and Aegean Seas. Each city-state was a distinct entity, independent from the others, with its own sovereign government and way of life. Often these cities fought amongst themselves for control of surrounding territory and to establish dominance over one another.

Finally, from all of these struggles, about a hundred years ago, two cities, Athens and Sparta, which had as yet not fought one another, having dominated their previous enemies (albeit for separate reasons), stood stronger than all others. And the rivalry between them began to simmer. The two societies could not have been more different. Sparta was a rigid military state. Its infantry, the most feared in all Greece, allowed Sparta to enslave the peoples in the neighboring lands and to establish dominance over the rest of the Peloponnesian Peninsula. From birth, each Spartan male was fashioned into a strapping instrument of cold, swift, brutal death. On the other hand, Athens was a democracy that had become the foremost trading center and naval power of the Greek world; its people enjoyed a lavish lifestyle in comparison to others, especially those living in the stagnant Spartan backwater, which shunned trade and contact with outsiders.

But then, roughly seventy years ago, the Persian army, the most powerful military force on earth, invaded mainland Greece. Now Sparta and Athens, as seemingly opposite as they were, banded together to lead the other cities against the invaders. Despite being far outnumbered and not without much sacrifice, over several years, the Greeks beat the foreign enemy away at Marathon, Thermopylae, Salamis, and finally, Plataea.

However, in the decades after the Persians were driven out, once more the divide between Sparta and Athens widened—this time to a jagged, gaping chasm. Sparta returned to building its military power and consolidating its hold over its surrounding territory. Under leadership of the influential politician Pericles, Athens rose to its Golden Age and became the commercial, cultural, and architectural marvel of the entire known world. And the Athenian political system, democracy, adopted by an increasing number of other city-states, was spreading quickly.

Finally, eleven years ago, fearing that Athens' growing power and influence would eventually destroy their own rigid way of life, the Spartans decided to attack. That summer, a Spartan army commanded by Archidamus, one of its two kings, marched on Athens, intent on putting the rival city's prideful residents in their place.

But the Athenians did not respond to the invasion as expected. Instead of racing out to meet the Spartans in open ground, where they risked being cut to ribbons, the Athenians, urged by Pericles, withdrew behind their massive fortified walls, which ran all around the city and continued four miles down to protect their seaport of Piraeus. And that whole summer, Athens held behind its fortifications, re-supplied by ship through Piraeus, the waters outside its three harbors patrolled by the powerful Athenian navy.

Then, as that summer drew to a close, Archidamus marched his army back home. The dry, hot weather was for fighting; and cold, wet winters were not suitable to keep troops out in the open. But more importantly, the Spartan king wanted to keep the Helots (the people inhabiting the village regions near Sparta) well reminded of their place, lest they be tempted to rebel against the small Spartan force that had remained to watch over the homeland. Hundreds of years previous, the Spartans had conquered the Helots and turned them into serfs, forcing them to give over most of the food grown on their arable land. But the Helots outnumbered the Spartans ten to one, and the cruel masters regularly unleashed their army to hunt down and massacre the most defiant Helots, thereby creating the terror among the slaves that kept them submitted.

The following fighting season, the Spartans invaded again, and again Athens held behind its walls, and Pericles was hailed as a genius. But that all unraveled in the third summer when plague, brought on some ship, broke out inside the once more besieged city, killing one-third of Athens' people, including Pericles himself. Yet defeat by the Spartans seemed a worse proposition than the deadly infestation, and Athens did not give up.

Now, into the space vacated by Pericles surged new men of influence; under their leadership, Athens pursued a different course —aggressive counterattack—using the navy to land troops in a series of lightning raids against outlying Spartan territory in the Peloponnese. Sparta responded by splitting its army into several smaller units to defend every corner of its far-flung dominion, and thus the Athenian troops were able to avoid an all-out battle with the whole Spartan force. For four years, this shift in strategy brought many Athenian victories—the greatest of all at the Island of Wasps, when the Athenians defeated the Spartans, taking 292 of them prisoner and shattering forever the myth that a Spartan soldier would never surrender, even in the face of certain death. However, more importantly, now the Spartan army, mindful of securing its own home, did not come to Athens.

But then, in the fifth year after Athens began its more aggressive prosecution of the war, the tables turned again. The rallying Spartans dealt a series of defeats to Athenian troops, most crushing of all when they massacred many of Athens' most experienced men in the process of overrunning the city of Amphipolis, an Athenian ally. This stunning defeat shocked and outraged the Athenian people, and they voted in favor of a return to the more cautious defensive strategy pursued when Pericles was at the helm.

Since the Spartans were winning again and with the renewed

lack of Athenian offensive forays against Spartan lands, within a year, King Archidamus reinvigorated the siege of the hated enemy's home. But Athens held that summer, the one after, and so far had not fallen this year, even though Archidamus, determined to breach the walls, had kept his troops out longer than usual.

And so, on the last morning of autumn, the thirty-three-year-old king stood in his tent, jaw clenched resolute as he prepared for one last assault before removing his army back to Sparta for the winter. The enormous brute stood six-foot-four and weighed 255 pounds. His dark, baboon-like features menaced under long, black, plaited hair and short beard.

Now Archidamus fastened on his golden bronze armor with its leather bindings: breastplate over his Spartan Red (deep blood-red) wool tunic and then greaves over his shins and knees. He picked up his polished bronze helmet (with a side-to-side, Spartan Red horsehair crest) and placed it on his head. He strapped on his thick leather belt; his short sword, meant for cleaving at close quarters, hung sheathed from its side. Last, he gathered his massive shield, a Spartan Red inverted "V" blazed across its shining bronze face. Then he strode towards and out the slit of the tent.

General Brasidas, forty, similarly dressed and armed for battle, waited for him outside (in the otherwise deserted camp) with two horses—a black stallion and a white stallion with gray spots. He was a tall and big man, but not as tall or as muscled as Archidamus. Like all other Spartan soldiers, though his sand-colored hair and pale skin were lighter than theirs, he groomed in the same manner as his king—long, plaited locks and short beard. It was said that it made a handsome man more so, and an ugly one terrifying, and a few men, like Brasidas, both more pleasing and more dreadful at the same time. The features on his rounded face, though clearly handsome as a whole, by themselves held an eerie cunning, betrayed most by cloudy yet piercing green eyes. His venom in combat matched his guile. He had led the surge that turned the war back the Spartans' way, including the battle of Amphipolis. And as such he commanded the absolute trust and respect of his fellow warriors, including his king.

Brasidas handed Archidamus the reins to the black stallion. They each mounted and then galloped away down a row of tents, kicking up the mud behind. The mammoth steeds pounded along as the two sinister horsemen rode, without a word between them, even as they reached the edge of the camp. Now they looked at, one hundred yards away, the back of the entire Spartan force, a hundred rows broad and deep. The soldiers had woken at five in the morning (three hours ago), eaten what for some would be their last meal, donned their armor, gathered their weapons, and marched out as one to where they stood now—in perfect formation, outside the range of the skilled enemy archers, ready to charge.

Five hundred yards further in the distance—across the open, shrubby ground—lay the outer bounds of Athens. The perimeter wall was thirty feet tall and eight feet thick, except near the top, where the wall (there a foot deep) fronted a chest-high protected walkway. The city's two broadest gateways, Dipylon to the left, Sacred to the right, lay directly ahead, both of them recessed so that any enemy, to reach their oak doors, would have to cross a walled courtyard surrounded by the perimeter wall's walkways, including those atop the square towers at the corners.

Atop the ramparts and on the ground behind the gates, the defenders of the city, twenty thousand strong, waited for the Spartan charge. At the start of the war, they had numbered thirty-five thousand, but plague, defeat, and even victory had culled a heavy toll.

The fair-skinned sons of Athens wore bronze breastplates over their white tunics with blue trim. Their shining bronze helmets were adorned with front-to-back crests of white horsehair. They were armed with sturdy short swords, eight-foot-long spears, and rocks collected to send over the side onto the enemy. The round faces of their shining bronze shields each bore a painted symbol to indicate membership in a particular troop. Snakes, bulls' heads, and horses were most common.

The thousand-strong corps of Scythian archers stood with the sons of Athens on the ramparts. The skilled service of these men from the steppes north of the Black Sea had been pledged to Athens in exchange for silver, but they still dressed and groomed in the distinctive manner of their native land. Long, black hair flowed out from under the backs of tan leather caps that each started at a point above center-crown and then wrapped down around their heads, leaving their bearded faces exposed only below the eyebrows. Their long-sleeved jackets (dyed bright green and covered with leopard-like spots) were cinched at the waist by black belts and hung down to mid-thigh, over matching trousers that tapered down to just above their ankles and tan leather boots.

The sons of Athens also manned the ground behind the gateways. In front of them, on the ground behind the Dipylon, stood the seven hundred hardy warriors from the town of Plataea, Athens' staunchest ally. Seventy years ago, as the Persians swept into southern Greece, among all the Greeks, only Athenians and Plataeans joined forces to meet them at Marathon. Together, despite being greatly outnumbered, standing shoulder-to-shoulder in their heavy armor, they crushed the Persian line, routing the invaders. That day, Athenians and Plataeans became brothers, in death and in victory. And when the present conflict began, it was an easy choice for them to side together, even though, eleven years after Marathon, the Spartans led a combined Greek force against the Persians in the final battle on the plain outside Plataea.

Athens was grateful for the Plataeans' loyalty. They, though few in number, were rugged and determined fighters. Over their brown tunics, they still wore the same dull-black armor and crestless helmets in which their grandfathers, then young men, had graced the field at Marathon. They fought with the same short swords and bore the same large shields—dull-black faces adorned with plump, mustard-yellow scorpions.

Demosthenes, one of Athens' ten generals, stood on the platform of the Dipylon Gateway's left front tower watching Archidamus and Brasidas (in the distance) canter past the last tent and out to join the assembled Spartan ranks. His six-foot-one frame carried his 220 pounds with utter grace. Even at forty, he was still a ruggedly handsome man with medium-length, shaggy, dark hair; angular features, dominated by a chiseled cleft chin; and dark, deep-set, intensely burning eyes. But Demosthenes also struck a commanding presence beyond that demanded by his impressive physical attributes. As one of its principal proponents, he had led the Athenian counteroffensive in the middle of the war, and his valor and brilliance had claimed the day for Athens at the Island of Wasps. But with the turning of fortune back to Sparta, he fell into disfavor, and though still a general with many supporters, ultimate command had ceded to the man now standing anxiously next to him.

General Nicias was almost fifty. He had thin lips; short, thinning, salt-and-sand hair; and an oval face, more lined than it should have been for a man of his age. His average body, too, looked tired and frail under its drooped shoulders. He had worshipped the living Pericles. And as the principal advocate (after Pericles' death) of the more defensive strategy, Nicias had been given supreme command of all the army when Athens decided to return to a cautious posture after the defeat at Amphipolis.

Alongside the two senior officers of Athens stood twenty-five-year-old Marathon, the dashing captain who was named after the great battle because his own grandfather had fought and died there. Physically, he resembled a younger and more handsome version of Demosthenes, the man he greatly admired as much as he despised Nicias. General Nicias' policies had shamed Athens and hurt the army's morale. Greek men always had fought invaders to expel them from every inch of sovereign territory. And Athenians especially, with their storied history of great military victories and vast wealth, were not meant to cower behind walls.

Out in the field, Archidamus and Brasidas arrived and trotted across the face of the assembled throng. And the deliberate yet fearsome rhythm filled the air of ten thousand long spears banging with one voice against the sides of ten thousand round shields. Three deafening clanks—a pause—and then three more deafening clanks continued as Archidamus and Brasidas arrived in front of the center of the formation, stopped the horses, and turned to face the troops. Then Brasidas held up his hand for the noise to end.

Immediately, all fell dead silent, except for the sound of the heavy breath of the two steeds, as Archidamus stared proudly at the Spartan war machine. Every one of his infantrymen was an equally impressive sight. In fact, he could not much tell one from the other, or him from them, except for the transverse crest on his helmet and the eight-foot, bronze-tipped spears in their hands. Their long, plaited hair flowed out from under the helmets (with front-to-back, Spartan Red horsehair crests) that covered their scowling faces. Their heavily muscled, armor-clad bodies stood strong and de-termined, broad swords hanging at their sides. And the soldiers all proudly bore massive shields with the same Spartan Red inverted "V" (which struck terror in the hearts of most enemies) blazed across every one of their shining bronze faces.

"Remember," Archidamus shouted into the quiet. "Remember all that you have done to prepare for this moment from the time that you were seven—when you first began your training. Remember the many battles that you have won since then. And do not forget as you fight today that grown men scream like babies calling for their mothers, when they feel Spartan swords upon their flesh."

He paused and then spoke again. "Now let us finish what we came here to do—so that we can return home as heroes!"

The Spartan horde, passions roused by their king, resumed the deafening rhythm of spear against shield. Archidamus and Brasidas dismounted, and each slapped his horse on the rear so that it would trot away behind the formation and back to the safety of the camp.

Archidamus and Brasidas turned towards Athens. Archidamus drew his sword and raised it above his head, and once more the banging stopped.

"Forward," shouted Archidamus, pointing his broad blade straight out in front of him at the enemy as he stepped ahead, with Brasidas at his side and the ranks of the ten thousand surging close behind.

General Nicias ran from atop the Dipylon's left front tower, all the way to the highest window at the back of the gateway's left rear tower. Then he leaned over its sill and called to Demosthenes, who now stood below, on the ground twenty yards behind the gateway's two doorways, at the head of five thousand men. "Demosthenes, here they come!"

Demosthenes nodded confidently back at Nicias to acknowledge the warning, and then he turned to his men; the seven hundred Plataean swordsmen at the front were resolved to meet the Spartans first if they should breach the heavy oak doors. "You are Athens' finest warriors. The enemy will attack strongest here at the Dipylon. We must hold them, no matter what."

"Yes, sir," the Plataeans chanted in reply, knowing all too well

what horrors Demosthenes dreaded, not least for Athens' defenseless noncombatants, who had taken anxious refuge high up on the
Acropolis in the glorious buildings atop the massive limestone hill
that rose above the center of the city. Plataea's gate had fallen nine
years earlier. With Plataea's perimeter protection neutralized, the
ten thousand Spartans had easily overwhelmed the two thousand
defenders and then proceeded to execute all of the town's
remaining inhabitants—including women and children. The seven
hundred who now stood in front of Demosthenes were saved only
because they were away from Plataea, having come to help guard
Athens under the mistaken belief that the Spartans would attack
there, instead of at their home. After the Persians were defeated on
the plain outside Plataea, all the Greeks (including the Spartans)
had sworn an oath that the town, for all time, would be held
sacred, immune from attack.

Out in the field, the Spartan juggernaut had split into two
separate brigades—each marching purposefully onward as a tight,
well-ordered, cohesive unit—closing steadily at an ever-quickening
pace. Archidamus led the larger brigade, six thousand men (sixty
across, one hundred deep), directly at the Dipylon Gateway. Brasidas led the smaller brigade, four thousand men (forty across, one
hundred deep), directly at the Sacred Gateway.

Soon each brigade shortened the distance from its goal to a
hundred yards. General Nicias, having returned to the platform
atop the Dipylon's left front tower, drew his sword and held it at his
side as he ordered the archers to come to the fore. The thousand-
strong Scythian corps stepped into place atop the front gateway

towers and across the wall-top. Then each pulled a single long-shafted, white-feathered arrow from the laden quiver hanging from the left side of his belt, placed it on his bow, and drew the string back as he angled his weapon upwards and away.

"Fire!" shouted Nicias, raising his sword straight above his head.

The archers loosened their fingers, the bowstrings snapped, and in perfect unison a thousand arrows sped into the air, whistling as they left to arc up into the sky and then descend some eighty yards in the distance.

"Shields up!" ordered Archidamus. Beginning with the first row and then rippling through to the back, the king and his men all raised their enormous shields above their heads, interlocked one with the other to form a canopy.

"Shields up!" ordered Brasidas, and his brigade raised their shields to make a shell.

The arrows landed on both brigades and, for the most part, hit where the Spartans had hoped. But the missiles that found their way through to the targets under, struck terribly. As the unfortunates fell, some wounded and some dead, their own comrades trampled them underfoot—without a care except to close the holes in the canopy where their friends had once stood—while yard after yard, one volley of incoming shafts after another, the Spartans bore steadily down on Athens.

Both Spartan brigades, shields still raised, reached the walls and stormed into the courtyards of the two gateways. Athenian soldiers cast spears and rolled stones down from atop the surrounding ramparts, inflicting more losses on the invaders than the

Scythian arrows had. But still, for the most part, the canopies of blood-red and shining bronze held, and the Spartans pressed on towards the oak.

Archidamus reached the Dipylon Gateway's doors; his brigade packed the courtyard wall-to-wall and extended all the way back, many yards beyond its mouth. Now, with the weight of thousands of comrades pushing them from behind, Archidamus and the others at the front began trying to force the portals down, even in the face of an intensified attack from above. Scythian archers had surged from the front of the wall-top onto the courtyard's ramparts to add their speeding shafts to the spears and stones already raining down.

Brasidas and his men reached the Sacred Gateway's portal, his brigade packing the smaller courtyard wall-to-wall and extending all the way back, a great number of yards beyond its mouth. Under assault from the skies, they pushed to break the door down, while some of their number entered the channel of water—it ran into the city on the courtyard's north side—in the hope that they could find a way through, under the walls. Captain Marathon and four thousand swordsmen, ready to do their duty, waited for Brasidas' men on the path inside, should the door break. Meanwhile, defenders (standing in the channel with long pikes) speared any enemy trying to sneak under the wall by the waterway.

Though barricaded from behind, the right door of the Dipylon strained and broke under the collective force of the Spartan horde, which stormed in over the shattered remains, led by Archidamus, sword drawn. Demosthenes, Plataeans thick at his side, rushed forward to meet them. Six yards inside the entrance, the two forces met with a thunderous crash from which many fell.

As the battle raged, the defenders of the Dipylon held their own, giving as good as they got and refusing to yield an inch more to the fearsome Spartans, even when the other portal broke, and the second wave of invaders flooded inside.

Archidamus and Demosthenes now stood face-to-face. The king had longed for the moment when he would destroy the man responsible for the humiliation suffered by the Spartans at the Island of Wasps. And he let fly with a furious series of overhead sword blows that the Athenian general blocked with his own blade, inches from his helmet.

The Spartan king, sensing that his adversary was open down low, swiftly thrust his weapon's point straight at Demosthenes' groin. But Demosthenes obstructed with his shield (painted on its face with the head of a bull) and then swung down sharply with his own sword atop Archidamus' outstretched blade. The intensity of the blow knocked the weapon loose from the Spartan's hand onto the ground.

Demosthenes swung hard overhead to finish, but Archidamus raised his shield to block; the force of Demosthenes' sword crashing against it almost buckled the Spartan king's knees. Then, before the Athenian general could swing on the king again, two Spartan captains, realizing the danger to their monarch, stepped in front to keep Demosthenes at bay, their sharpened metal clashing hard with his.

Now, as the fighting continued all around, Archidamus realized that his plan had failed. He had hoped to sweep swiftly into Athens, once the doors had been breached. But the resistance on the ground behind the Dipylon had proven more able than he had expected, holding most of his men up too long in the courtyard, with no way forward in sight. Already too many Spartans lay underfoot, and if he kept his men in the passage—though their shell of shields still held fairly well—eventually the relentless torrent of projectiles from the ramparts would turn it into a slaughter-house.

Determined to prevent the cost from rising much higher, Archidamus gave the order to retreat. The command went calmly rippling through the ranks, all the way to the back row. Without breaking battle array, the whole brigade, starting at the rear, began moving back, even as the fighting continued at the front and the sky continued to shower death.

As Archidamus and the foremost of his brigade backed out of the Dipylon's doorways into the courtyard, Demosthenes ordered the defenders to hold and reform ranks at their original position inside. The Athenian general knew that in the channel's frenzy his men could suffer a friendly death from the objects raining from the ramparts.

Either the Plataeans did not hear Demosthenes' order; or, hungering to avenge the atrocity committed on their town, they did not honor it. As the Plataeans surged through after the retreating Spartans, the first of them fell victim to missiles from atop, before their allies up high could make out that they had entered the courtyard.

Demosthenes and the Athenian swordsmen followed the Plataeans through the doorways and stayed lodged behind them against the enemy, even as the Spartans backed all the way out of the corridor. Now the Plataeans reached the mouth of the court-yard, and Demosthenes, following close, again shouted for them to stop. It was unwise to face the Spartan army in open ground, without the advantage of the narrow channel to control the flow of their numbers and disrupt their formation.

The Plataeans did not break off, and (still backed by their trailing Athenian brothers) they chased the front line of the retreating invaders past the courtyard's mouth, some seventy yards further on. There Archidamus' brigade joined again with that of Brasidas, which having failed to pierce the Sacred Gateway by door or by water channel, also had retreated to avoid sustaining heavier casualties. Now the Spartans (reformed into one massive, tight, cohesive unit) halted their retreat and, in their preferred formation, cut the onrushing front line of Plataeans to shreds. Even the archers atop Athens' ramparts could not help, fearing that their shafts would fall on friend as well as foe.

Again Demosthenes ordered retreat, and this time the remain-ing Plataeans obeyed, withdrawing towards the city with their Athenian brothers. Meanwhile, the Spartans, having proven their point, began backing away towards their tents, with their shields raised to protect against renewed assault from white-feathered arrows.

The Spartans halted at their original line outside their camp. And they stood in ranks there, just as they had before the start of the battle—beyond Scythian range, some five hundred yards from Athens' perimeter. But now the Spartans numbered nine thousand, instead of ten.

The defenders of Athens, as before, manned the city's ramparts. But now, instead of waiting behind the Dipylon's two portals, Demosthenes, joined by Marathon, stood with his men in the courtyard in front, filling it to the mouth. Behind them, carpenters worked feverishly to restore the fallen doors, while the wounded and the dead (every Spartan assured of the second condition by the entire blade-length of an Athenian knife) were recovered from the ground all around.

All day this standoff persisted, always capable of bursting again into combat. But it never did. Then, as dusk came and fell into full night, the two sides, unlike any other day, remained where they were. Now the Athenians mounted burning torches all across their wall-top and towers, and the flickering lights from Athens were bright. The Spartan camp, nestled at the base of the mountains to the northwest of Athens, contrary to previous nights, remained dark; however, the outline of the Spartan army's unyielding assembly was vaguely discernible by the silver light of the full moon.

About three in the morning, the moon began to set, and it no longer gave off illumination sufficient for the defenders of Athens to discern even the general outline of the Spartan ranks. In fact, the Spartans would have to come far closer than their present position to be seen approaching.

An hour later, nature's nightlight having receded further, a bustling commotion could be heard from the direction of the

Spartan line. Now the defenders readied for the Spartan horde to suddenly burst towards them out of the dark, into the glow of Athens' torches, their furthest effect emitting only eighty yards beyond city limits.

The noise continued for the next hour. Then it subsided. Still the enemy had not come. Then, just before six, the dawn's hazy light revealed the mystery. The Spartan camp was gone (not a single invader or tent remaining), and the Spartan army was marching over the gentle coastal range to leave back to their own home.

This fighting season was over.

Chapter Three

THE DREAM LIVES

Orion, young Champion of Elis, and Cadmus, his puny best friend, lived together on a farm at the base of the rolling hills ten miles to the northeast of their city proper. Their modest house was a one-story structure with thick stone walls, sturdy timber doorposts and rafters, oak-shuttered windows, a sloped clay-tile roof, and covered porches at the front and back. There were only five rooms inside of it—two bedrooms, a living room, a kitchen, and a storeroom for tools and supplies.

The vegetable garden grew to the left of the house, and a small barley field grew on the right side. The sheep pen, surrounded by a hip-level stone wall and wooden gate, sat at the back of the house, just below the gentle grass slopes on which the flock grazed by day.

Cadmus was born and raised on the property. His parents had given it to him when they moved into the heart of Elis, almost four years previous, so that his father could pursue the profession he always had wished for himself—maker of fine pottery. Cadmus' parents had asked him to join them—at first and then a year later as their new venture flourished under the green cloth roof of their stall in the middle of the Agora's rectangular dirt floor. But Cadmus chose to stay in the only life he had ever known.

Orion, on the other hand, came to the farm from something very different. He was born into a wealthy family, living in the best district of Elis, in a grand house, complete with servants. His father had made a fortune in olive oil. Its uses were many: cooking, lighting lamps, and rubbing over the body. And Orion's father's groves, on the most fertile land to the west of the city, produced large quantities of the best oil because one of his many workers had developed a new and secret way of pressing the nectar out of the fruit.

Orion's brother, two years older than him, always had been the easy child. He never stepped outside the defined bounds; and, unlike Orion, he flowed naturally to "proper" habits. But, from the start, even as a young boy, Orion's will clashed with that of his parents, who saw it as their job to mold him into an image of themselves so that he could live the same life as they had, ruled by fear and a need for certainty. His parents employed whatever means were necessary (including frequent switching with a thin, wet branch across the back of his legs) to break their "ungrateful" son's stubborn, independent, adventurous spirit.

As Orion grew into a teenager and his body became stronger from regular exercise, the switch gave way to a more insidious form of persuasion. Now they controlled him by his thoughts and emotions, equating all activities that did not fit into their vision of the world with failure and worthlessness and by conditioning all approval and acceptance of Orion upon his unquestioning compliance with their wishes for his life. "If you are a failure, no one will want to have anything to do with you, and you will lose all your friends. We just have your best interests at heart."

At fourteen, as expected, Orion's brother joined the family business in the shop under the south perimeter colonnade of the Agora. There he learned the art of haggling and sharp business practice from their father, who sought always to extract every advantage from others, regardless of circumstance. Two years later, when he turned the same age, Orion joined them there, though not nearly as happily. He had wanted to work the olive groves, to be outside with nature, among the people who farmed it. They reflected its simple honesty. But Orion's father refused. Physical labor was beneath his son's station—as was any association with the workers. And Orion's father decided that Orion would have to give up his athletic training, too, no matter how much Orion dreamed of becoming Olympic Champion someday. There would be no time for that now. "Besides, Orion, such aspirations are ridiculous. The games have been ended by the war, and they will not be held again while you are still young enough to compete."

Thus, for the next five years, Orion (his hopes and dreams dead, swayed by his parents' promises of a rich life and the basic need of any child to gain approval) worked at the Agora shop. But he had no desire or ability for harsh practices. And he conducted his duties with too much generosity towards the less fortunate, arousing the ire of his father and brother, who more and more oversaw every detail of his tasks, sapping his every ounce of confidence and initiative. The routine, boredom, and feelings of incompetence ate away what little passion he had left, and he felt trapped in someone else's life.

But then, when Orion was nineteen, everything changed. The Hellanodikes announced the First Elean Games, and Orion decided to compete. His parents, unhappy with this choice, said they were ashamed of him and that he would not be welcome in their home any longer if he participated in sport of any kind. They expected Orion to cave to their will and beg to stay. Instead, Orion took up Cadmus' invitation to live and train on the farm. The two young men had been best friends since Cadmus had beaten Orion at boxing when they were both ten (before Orion sprouted stronger and Cadmus stopped growing) and Cadmus took great pride in helping Orion prepare for the upcoming contest. A month later, Orion won the First Elean Games.

After that, he and Cadmus decided that he should stay living on the farm. Immediately, Orion settled easily into his new life, completely at peace, training for the next athletic contest and working in nature at the same time. Cadmus was glad for the company (he had been lonely there since his parents left) and for the help. The vegetable garden and barley field needed tending, and the sheep required considerable attention even apart from the fact that someone always had to watch over the flock—by day, to prevent them from wandering off as they grazed on the hills behind the house, and at night, in their corral, to keep them safe from the wolves that descended from the mountains in packs when the weather turned colder.

❧

Months after Orion had defeated Hipponax to win his third consecutive Elean Games, on the same day and at the same time (around five in the morning) as the Spartans finished packing their camp to withdraw from Athens, Orion and Cadmus were underneath the back porch of their house. Wrapped in wool blankets, the two friends sat on wooden chairs as they looked out at the sheep pen and the rolling hills, rising just behind. Each held his sturdy, six-foot-long beech-wood staff, Orion in his right hand and Cadmus in his left. Wolves had come the evening before to cull from their neighbor's bleating flock.

Orion (exhausted from a hard day of work and training) was having trouble staying awake, despite Cadmus' efforts to keep him from falling asleep by rambling on and on with his usual set of notoriously bad jokes.

Orion nodded and drifted away.

Suddenly, he saw the gods gathered in the Great Meeting Hall of their magnificent home atop Olympus, the tallest mountain in Greece. The massive rectangular temple (with no walls, open to the air on every side) sat alone, occupying the whole summit. The rest of the white-marble palace complex, the twelve Olympians' private quarters, consisted of one big circular building, which fitted like a

snug ring around the cone of the peak, just below the summit. Twelve staircases (one from each of the rooms) ascended to join the Great Meeting Hall's rectangular perimeter, around which twelve Corinthian columns stood evenly spaced to support the peaked roof.

In the center of the Great Meeting Hall's vast floor, an expressionless golden statue of Zeus (human in shape but twice the size of a man) sat on a golden throne. In this form, the leader of the gods could mostly be described as a tall and robust old man. His long hair and beard resembled the thick mane of a lion. His face, too, dominated by the bridge of his unyielding nose, reminded one of the king of beasts.

Right in front of him, Zeus was looking into a shallow round pool made of shining silver; its twelve-foot diameter was filled with crystal-clear water. Ten similar golden statues stood facing the silver pool, evenly spaced to form a complete circle around it with Zeus' throne. These were the other gods who lived on Olympus: Demeter, goddess of the harvest; Dionysus, god of wine; Apollo, sun god; Artemis, goddess of the hunt; Aphrodite, goddess of love; Hermes, messenger god; Hestia, goddess of the home; Ares, god of war; Hera, goddess of marriage; Athena, goddess of wisdom.

Now, just as the gilded statues had witnessed the desperate struggle to save Athens, the image of the entire departing Spartan army starting into the mountains that sat behind the now-vanished camp of red tents flashed at them all through the sparkling water on the silver bottom of the pool.

Suddenly, the statue of Zeus morphed from gold to flesh and

blood, still twice the size of a man; his skin separated from the armrests, out of which it had previously flowed as if Zeus and the throne were one.

"This will not do," grumbled Zeus, brow furrowed as he stood up. "The Spartans have driven Greece into a sorry state. These are bad times—far too much turmoil."

The golden statue of Ares, god of war, morphed to flesh and blood. But unlike Zeus, whose transformation began with his feet on up through his head, Ares fleshed from crown to base. In human form, he appeared as a strapping thirty-year-old man. He wore his long, black hair braided like the Spartans. His aggressive face featured a protruding brow and short beard.

"Zeus, don't be so dramatic," he said sarcastically. "There have always been wars, and there will always be wars. It is the natural condition of mortals. They will always find something to fight about. I remember when…"

The golden statue of Athena, goddess of wisdom, came to life in similar fashion to Zeus. She was slightly plump. But she also was tall and elegant. Her long, curly, brown hair was wrapped in a tight bun behind. Her round face, complex yet simple, always seemed both worried and happy at the same time.

"No, Ares," she interrupted sternly, "most mortals have peace in their hearts. It is only those you have infected with your lust for war that conquer and destroy."

"Don't preach to me, Athena," Ares replied. "You are a hypocrite. You are not so different from me. Your hands are far from clean. Did I complain when time after time you backed the other side against Sparta? You could have stayed out of it, you know, if you are so against fighting. And now you are just upset because Athens will fall by this time next year. What a sore loser you are."

"How blind you are," Athena responded heatedly. "I am not like you. I give courage to peaceful mortals who are forced to defend themselves. But you—you twist the minds of your followers to wage this evil campaign of aggression, simply so they can impose their ways on everyone else."

"Stop it," Zeus said, his patience thin. "Stop it right now—the two of you. There have been more than enough arguments between mortals and among us gods."

Ares and Athena stopped but still glared at each other as Zeus continued.

"I have thought much about these matters, and I have made a decision," said Zeus, sighing. "We will revive the Olympic Games in the hope that they will restore peace to the mortal world. It has been too long since they were last held."

"But," Ares protested.

Zeus did not let him finish.

"Let me explain," Zeus continued, lecturing on facts well known to the others as a firm declaration of his will, rather than out of any need to educate. "I am sure you all remember that before Greece was so divided and in such chaos, the Olympic Games were very popular. One and all, throughout the entire land, observed a great truce to hold them. Often, when there were conflicts, the truce turned into lasting peace since everyone could meet without fear to enjoy the competition; and, in that setting, they put aside their differences for good."

"But things have changed much since then," Ares added quickly, his stomach churning at even the prospect of peace. He loved suffering and delighted in the massacre of men, and now he intended to cut off any possibility that Zeus would help the mortals end their bitter conflict. But he also knew that stubborn Zeus would not relinquish his idea if challenged directly. Ares' best hope was to persuade the leader of the gods that his goal could not be achieved by such means. "Life and politics are far more complicated than before. Such an old idea as the Olympic Games could never work in today's world."

"Then you should have no objection," replied Zeus, wise to Ares' scheme, "when I command all of Greece to declare a truce to participate."

Ares was about to contest when the golden statue of the sun god came to life, like the war god, beginning at the crown. Haughty Apollo was a stunningly handsome youth of twenty. He had short, blonde hair. His long and lean body, though fit, was meant for leisure and pleasure, not for work or war. And, as such, it was not as heavily muscled as Ares' deep, powerful layers. "But I object!" Apollo interjected contentiously.

"I expect no less from you, Apollo," replied Zeus, struggling to restrain the deep anger he held towards his irreverent son.

"Keep your sarcasm for others," Apollo snapped, his own long-standing resentment for domineering Zeus bubbling to the surface. "My point is that we should not meddle so deeply in human matters. Helping one mortal here and another there is fine. But now—now you would command the whole of Greece to follow this whim of yours. Your pride has risen beyond your reason."

"You should stop talking, Apollo," barked Zeus. "You are making a fool of yourself."

"I will not," Apollo responded, calmer now that he was taking the conversation in the direction he wanted. "Too long have I waited in silence and watched how you have conducted yourself as leader of us gods. You always just do what you want. You never really give us a say in matters."

"That is a lie," shouted Zeus, angrily responding to the sun god's attack. "Everyone is allowed to speak his mind here."

"Yes, that is true," responded Apollo. "But we never get to decide. You have the final word on everything, whether we agree with your choices or not. And that is not how gods should conduct their affairs. Maybe it is time that another one of us, with clearer vision, take over the reins of Olympus."

"Someone like you, I suppose?" asked Zeus, with even greater sarcasm than before. He knew what burned in Apollo's heart.

"And why not me?" replied Apollo, eagerly.

"Is there nothing you do not covet for your own?" asked Zeus, pleased at how easily he had exposed Apollo's true motive. Now that it was in the open, apparent to the other gods, he could both attack it and achieve his own purpose in a single swoop. "I know what greed lies inside of you. For years, you have sought a way to challenge my authority so that you could take it. But I warn you— you are well advised to save your rebellion for another occasion. I am firmly set on restoring the Olympic Games among the mortals, and I will not allow your pathetic attempt to steal what is not yours, to distract me from my purpose here today."

"Against that, we are firmly set," Ares chimed in. He and Apollo, albeit for different reasons, were clearly now allied in an unspoken pact that each would grant the other his desire if together they could defeat Zeus, especially on something that seemed so important to him. "If you insist on commanding these games, you will force us to remove you."

"You minnows!" shouted Zeus, so angrily that the home of the gods shook on its foundation. "How dare you threaten! This alliance of yours is but a sorry joke. What can the two of you do to me?"

"We are not alone," said Apollo. "Hermes will stand with us. And the others will soon follow. We are all tired of your commands."

"Which side do you choose, Hermes?" Zeus asked, with little assurance in his voice as he turned his attention away from Ares to look directly into the eyes of the statue of the messenger god.

Hermes morphed to flesh and blood. But, unlike any of the others, his thirty-year-old humanity began at the middle and then rippled out to each extreme. Then, with a blank expression on his cynical face, he walked over to stand with Ares and Apollo, less robust than the former and more so than the latter.

"Poor Hermes," said Zeus, glaring at the messenger god with disdain as he realized that Apollo already had secretly seduced susceptible Hermes to back him when he made his push for power. "You always try to extract something for yourself from every situation. What sweet, little temptations has Apollo been whispering in your eager ears? What he must have promised you in exchange for your support! Do you really expect him to deliver?"

Hermes (acknowledging the point but not to the extent that it made a difference) raised his eyebrows at Zeus but would not answer.

"Who else stands with these traitors?" asked Zeus, angrily looking around the circle of gilded statues.

They did not respond.

"I am with Zeus," Athena said, resolute and proud, hoping that it would spur others to follow her.

But none did.

"Who besides Athena will back me?" asked Zeus, getting no better from them than before.

"Enough, old man," shouted Apollo, sensing that this was the right moment to press his challenge. "Renounce the games or be removed."

"I will do neither," replied Zeus, angrily, and again the earth rumbled under the powerful vibration of his deep voice. "Now be quiet and crawl back into your holes before I strike you down."

Suddenly, Ares and Apollo, from head to tail, morphed into two giant cobras, each twice the size of a man, like their human forms. Then the two cobras raised the front halves of their bodies off the cool marble floor and fanned out their swaying heads wide—dark, beady eyes narrowing to focus on Zeus and Athena, who now stood together.

Hermes, starting with his belly, slowly changed himself band by band into a long, thin, colorful (black, yellowish-cream, and red), venomous coral snake. Then he coiled low to the ground, his slender forked tongue darting in and out.

The faces of the previously expressionless statues of the other gods were now afraid, but none dared move. The water in the pool turned from crystal clear to cloudy. And it bubbled steamy hot and turbulent as it threatened to surge over the side onto the floor. The spirit of the twelfth Olympian resided there, Zeus' absent brother, Poseidon, god of the seas.

Ares hissed and slithered towards Athena. She stood to face his challenge, a shield growing out of her left hand and a spear out of her right.

Apollo darted forward at his father. Zeus came to meet the giant cobra, his hands growing two glowing swords shaped like lightning bolts.

Hermes, seeing Zeus' power, reconsidered his choice and abandoned his alliance with Apollo and Ares; without advancing, Hermes instantly changed back from flesh to a golden statue of a coral snake.

As Ares reached Athena, his massive serpent's head loomed above her. He bared his fangs to strike. Athena raised her shield to parry, but the force of the cobra's lunge sent her flying and then skating across the slick marble floor until she landed against one of the tall, white columns at the outer edge of the Great Meeting Hall.

Apollo and Zeus met head on, the sun god viciously whipping and jabbing his poison-drenched incisors at his father. But Zeus dodged and slashed, slicing off large portions of the serpent's scales. Wounded, Apollo retreated for a moment to weigh his next move.

Ares slid over to Athena. She rose just in time to defend herself. Over and over, he leapt spitefully at her as she stood with the column pressed against her back, jabbing and parrying, barely holding him off.

Next to the stormy pool, Apollo, having gathered himself, lunged at Zeus again. Zeus dodged and, blades swirling, cut Apollo, this time deeper. Frightened and bleeding, he slithered away to the edge of the hall to escape down the stairs to his quarters. But Zeus, eyes blazing with fire, rushed over and reached to block the wounded snake's path before he could slip out.

"Zeus, wait!" exclaimed Apollo, quickly changing back from cobra to human form. Surely, Zeus would be more likely to take pity and spare him if he looked like a mortal rather than the most reviled of all creatures. "We should compromise."

"I do not compromise with reptiles," Zeus declared, still counting Apollo at his essence, regardless of appearance. Then he moved closer, his two jagged blades of light churning the air.

"Perhaps you should reconsider," Apollo said, pointing over behind Zeus to Ares and Athena.

Zeus, keeping one eye on Apollo, turned his head to look. Ares held Athena, still alive but helpless, in his fangs. Her weapons lay on the marble.

"What kind of compromise?" asked Zeus, as the fire died from his eyes, and they returned to deep blue. Athena would meet a terrible end if he did not strike a bargain.

Suddenly, the golden statue of Hestia, goddess of the home, well-skilled at bringing calm to her fellow gods, sprang to life all at once. She always chose to appear as an old woman with long, unkempt, gray hair and skin hanging loosely from the bones of her haggard face and dried, spent body. But this outer shell was countered by her nature, which, after time, made her seem almost pleasing to look at.

"You all pursue a course," she said with her soothing voice "that would destroy Olympus. Such high stakes are not wise for either side, especially when the outcome is as uncertain as it is here."

"What would you have us do?" Apollo asked, little hope in his tone.

"Let Zeus choose one mortal," Hestia said, "to go forth and convince Athens, Sparta, and all the other cities to declare a truce and hold the games. Then we can all sit back, without exercising any further influence, and allow man's true nature to decide his own fate."

"But that does not resolve our problems here on Olympus," Apollo scowled.

"I am not done," Hestia answered. "If the chosen mortal can revive the games and restore peace, then Zeus shall remain in charge. But if not, then you will take over leadership from Zeus."

"I will not make such a bargain," Zeus exclaimed. "I rule here, now and forever."

"What's the matter, Zeus?" Apollo taunted. "Are you afraid that you are wrong?"

Zeus' eyes began to glow red again. Then he looked once more at Athena, trapped in the cobra's mouth. Ares' incisors were pressing into her body. Any deeper and they would puncture.

"I agree," Zeus replied, eyes cooling to blue. His blades of light retracted and disappeared into his hands as he stepped back and away from smirking Apollo.

"Now let her go, Ares," Zeus commanded.

Ares dropped Athena from his mouth, and she hit the ground with a thud. Then, slowly, beginning with his feet on through to the top of his head, he turned back to human form. Next to him, Athena rose gingerly as she passed her hand over where Ares had pressed his fangs into her ribs. The fight had left her battered but not punctured.

"Whom will you select, Zeus?" Ares asked contemptuously, little expecting that anyone could achieve the goal upon which they had staked everything.

"You mock too soon, Ares," said Zeus, confidently. "I have the perfect mortal in mind."

"I doubt that," replied Apollo. "But tell us anyway. Who is he?"

"Orion of Elis," Zeus said emphatically.

"The sheepherder?" questioned Apollo, in disbelief.

"Precisely," replied Zeus, more certain than before.

"Come now, Zeus," laughed Apollo. "You make it too easy for my side with this pitiful choice. He is not even one of the Hellano-dikes."

"Certainly he is not, but he is much more than that," Zeus responded. "He is a great athletic champion who personifies the highest ideals of the Olympic Games—tough competition for the pure love of it, unshakable respect for fairness, and great compassion for others."

"That simpleton has no ambition," Apollo replied. "He craves no power. And he is fully incapable of cold calculation without regard for justice. Clearly, such a lack of character does not make for greatness."

"Orion is perfect to undertake this noble quest," interjected Athena, forcefully. "Only one of such high virtue can have any hope of restoring peace when the world is in such disarray."

"Still, even if you are right about those things," Ares added, "there is something about this mortal that neither of you has considered—which if you had, may well have altered the fervor with which you favor him."

"And what is that?" questioned Athena, worried by Ares' obvious confidence.

"Patience, Athena," replied Ares, brimming self-satisfied as ever. "For that, you will have to wait and see. But do not worry. It is just a matter of time before it becomes apparent."

Chapter Four

WOLVES

Orion stirred, and then he jerked awake, still sitting, wrapped in his wool blanket, in the chair under the back porch of the farmhouse. But now it was morning, the sun just rising behind the mountains away to the east, beyond the hills and the sheep milling around in the corral. Cadmus' chair was empty, his wool blanket draped over, ends hanging down onto the dirt floor.

Orion shook his head to clear the fog.

"Here, take this," said Cadmus, walking up behind, out of the kitchen, with two steaming cups of tea in his hands, one offered to Orion. "The wolves never came, so I let you sleep. You must have been really tired. You were tossing around and talking to yourself."

"Thank you," Orion said, reaching to receive his cup.

Cadmus walked forward and leaned up against the timber post at the front edge of the porch, his back to Orion as he surveyed the flock and the view further on. "We better keep them in their pen again today. Letting them loose on the hill is not…"

"I had a vision last night," interrupted Orion. He was sure from the moment he woke. It was too different and too real to have been a dream.

"You had a what?" Cadmus blurted as he whipped around to face Orion.

"A vision," he replied confidently. "Zeus came to me in my sleep and commanded me to revive the Olympic Games in the hope they will bring lasting peace."

Then Orion explained all he experienced, and Cadmus listened carefully, realizing from Orion's face and from the tone of his voice that he was serious.

"So you had a dream?" Cadmus asked, still confused, straining to make sense of it all. "Is that what you are trying to tell me?"

"It wasn't a dream," said Orion, standing up from his chair. "It was a vision. Zeus spoke to me. I have to go to the Hellanodikes. Can you watch the sheep?"

"Yes, of course I can, but are you sure it wasn't just a dream?" replied Cadmus, surprised by the sudden and extreme turn of events. "Maybe you should think about it for a few days, to be completely certain, before you tell anyone else." Cadmus was hoping that if he could delay Orion, time would bring him to his senses. But Orion continued to insist that Zeus had chosen him to revive the Olympic Games. Then Cadmus challenged him more directly and more resolutely, and the two argued heatedly back and forth, and still Orion held firm. In the end, Cadmus gave up trying to convince his friend. Since parting with his family, Orion always, in important matters, fiercely defended his beliefs. He was determined never to feel uncertain of himself again, once he had, as in this case, decided on a path.

✄

The ten Hellanodikes were appointed for life from among the elder members of the two Elean families who could trace their origins back to Pelops, the mortal founder of the Olympic Games. It was assumed that his descendants would be the best guardians of the spirit and ideals of the grand event, and for many generations they were. But of late, the offices had fallen to men with less character, who cared more for their own aggrandizement and being pandered to than for serving their intended purpose. These men viciously guarded their position of entitlement as the sole voice of the games, attacking anyone whom they perceived as threatening their influence. This included Orion who, as three-time champion of the Elean contests, was becoming far too popular for their liking. A fact punctuated just months ago when the crowd stormed the Agora ring to congratulate him, pushing Solorchus (the fat Chief Hellanodike with ruffled hair and beard) into the mud.

The Hellanodikes met to hear petitions relating to the business of the Olympic Games at the Olympic Office, a circular hall with a high ceiling, located a block south of Elis' Agora. On the inside of its one large room, halfway up its smooth, white walls, a painted olive garland ran all around, ending at both sides of the wide dark-wood door. Now Orion stood in the middle of the open floor relating his sacred quest to the ten stern older men in purple royal robes. They were sitting evenly spaced around the hall's perimeter in ornately carved chairs, complete with armrests and deep-olive-colored seat cushions.

"And you really expect us to believe this preposterous story?" asked Solorchus, cynical as usual. "If Zeus wanted to revive the Olympic Games, he would have come to us, not you. We will not dispatch the heralds. Now is not the time. Sparta already has refused the truce twice."

"Then give me your blessing, and I will convince Sparta and Athens and everyone else to participate," offered Orion. His task would be far easier with their stamp of approval. Then, at least, he would be allowed to carry the staff (engraved near each tip with a dove holding an olive twig in its beak) borne by the heralds as a symbol of their official status. Without it, he would have more than the usual trouble persuading anyone that the games should indeed take place.

"We will do no such thing," shouted Solorchus, rising threateningly from his seat. "This meeting is over."

Despite Solorchus' pronouncement and succeeding demands that he depart, Orion refused to leave the Olympic Office. Instead, he pleaded and argued an hour longer. But the Hellanodikes did not change their minds. Eventually, it was clear (even to determined Orion) that they would never cede. Frustrated and angry, he stormed towards the exit. "I don't care what you say. I have a direct order from Zeus. I don't need you. I will revive the games myself!"

"And I warn you," Solorchus shouted as Orion burst out of the door, "there will be consequences if you even mention this ludicrous idea to anyone else!"

❧

Immediately, Orion returned to the farm and began packing to leave for the lands over the mountains to the east of Elis. Cadmus, having repeatedly tried and failed to dissuade Orion, decided that he would join his friend. Neither of them ever had traveled away from their hometown before, and the long journey would be too lonely and hard for Orion to endure without company.

The only thing standing in their way was finding someone to take care of the farm while they were gone. So they asked massive Hipponax, expecting that he of all people, being a friend (outside the wrestling ring) and loving sport as he did, would be willing to help. But he refused. Sixteen years ago, when he was nineteen, the big-boned giant with the enormous barrel chest had been an official herald. And now, despite his doubts that the gods had really appeared to Orion, he insisted on going along to show his friends the way. His only concern was getting permission from his wife, five feet tall and one-third his weight. But she gave it easily.

Next, Orion asked his younger cousin, Aeneas. He was seventeen with shoulder-length, black hair and a smooth, innocent face, similar to Orion's. Aeneas looked up to Orion and wanted to follow in his footsteps as an athletic champion, even though his body (only five-foot-ten, skinny, without muscles) bore little resemblance to his older relative's. He had been ill, when he was a baby, with the same fever that took his father to the grave. His mother, whom he resembled, nursed her only child back to life, and as he grew to a young man, she continued to worry for his health, jumping to care for him at even the slightest sign of a cold. Afraid that he would be injured, she had not been happy when, a year ago, Aeneas told her that Orion had agreed to begin training him. And she was even less so now, after Aeneas told her that he was joining Orion on his travels. Desperately, she begged and pleaded with him to stay, not calmed by her son's loving explanations of why he had to go. Zeus had called Orion to a noble quest. And Aeneas would help Orion fulfill his duty.

Two days later, Aeneas walked out of the house where he lived with his mother into the wide dirt street, lined with similar mud-brick homes; each one-story structure had its walls plastered over white and was covered by a clay-tile roof. He was on his way to join the three other travelers on the farm, from where they would start the journey the next morning.

His mother followed him out through the wide front door. Grabbing hold, she hugged him tight. "My Son, I am so proud of you. Come home safely." She had wanted to beg him to stay. But she knew he would not. Instead, she chose to send him off with an expression of love that in some way might protect him, by giving him strength, if he fell into danger in the strange lands far away.

"Thank you, Mother, I will," Aeneas replied, returning the embrace; tears in his own eyes, he was pained by her pain and by the fact that he had to leave her, despite the ample arrangements he had made for her care. Then he tried softly to break away. But she clung to him, not wanting to release him, ever.

"I must go now," Aeneas whispered, gently prying her hands away. "Don't worry. I'll be back before you know it."

Reluctantly, she loosened her arms and let go. Then, sobbing, she watched as her one pride and joy walked away down the street. Aeneas was smiling reassuringly as he glanced back—with vision blurred by his own tears.

Soon he was gone.

❧

Cadmus' parents would care for their former home while their son was away. And so, on the afternoon that the travelers gathered at the farm, Cadmus' parents left one of the young apprentices in charge of their Agora stall and came there too. Everyone stayed up late into the night, eating and talking in the kitchen, too excited to sleep. But finally they all did except for Cadmus' father. He kept an eye on the sheep.

The four travelers woke at sunrise, quickly ate breakfast, and said their farewells. Then, watched by Cadmus' parents from under the back porch, they walked past the sheep pen and up over the crest of the first hill behind the house, illuminated by golden rays. Each wore a beige wool tunic; a black wool cloak over it; a snug, black wool cap; and long, tan soft-leather boots that rose to just below the knees. On their backs, each strung, with black leather straps, a dark-brown leather pouch for water; a rolled-up wool blanket; and a small, light wooden box of food. In their hands, every one of them carried a staff, though none of the six-foot-long woods bore the official emblem of their cause.

The four travelers turned and waved, and then they disappeared down the other side of the first hill, from there heading across the rest of the rolling mounds onto the shrubby plain that would carry them to the mountains, many miles to the east. All their destinations lay beyond this range, including Athens, which they had decided to visit first.

By the end of the next day, at dusk, they got to the base of the range at the end of the flat. The first peak, shrouded in haze, loomed four thousand feet above them. There, on the ground below it, they made camp among a clump of thirteen forty-foot-tall trees, bushy thick with green leaves. And before long, a dense fog descended all around them. Only their fire kept it away.

The following morning, the four Eleans waited for the thick mist to lift higher, and then they hiked up the long, steep, stony, shrub-covered slope to the hard rock summit above. There, they rested for a while. Hipponax was out of breath from the climb, and already everyone's feet hurt, none of them being used to that much walking.

An hour later, they started across the rest of the range. A wide series of gentle grades and sharp inclines, some grassy and others stony and rocky, most dotted with tall mountain pines. And as they trudged deeper in, the fog never lifted higher than fifty feet above their heads, descending to encase them every night. And always the howling winter wind swept low through the whole landscape, biting past their wool, which was often drenched by the same freezing showers that wetted their boots.

Yet, despite all this, spirits were high. Their mission was far too important to let such trivialities as bad weather get in the way, especially when Cadmus and Hipponax, as always, provided such good entertainment for everyone with their constant banter, back and forth, thrusting and parrying, neither able to pierce the other's thick skin.

Halfway across the range, a week after they started into the mountains, the four Eleans came to the edge of a cliff. A huge wooded gorge lay below them—a thousand feet deep and three miles long, from right to left. Its stony ground—steep banks and twenty-foot-wide base—was covered by big trees with dark-black bark and wide branches. And all of the trees were dressed atop in autumn-colored leaves, bright reds and yellows.

It was now late in the day. The wind was whipping stronger and more biting than usual, and the fog had started coming down to the ground. So the four Eleans, to gain valued shelter, hiked down to the flat bottom of the gorge, chased by the thick white, rolling quickly behind them. Now Orion and his companions scampered around under the trees (their tops already being enveloped by the fog) looking for somewhere to settle. Before long, seventy yards to the left of where they arrived on the base, they found a basin-shaped hollow. Its moss-covered banks rounded six feet down, gently bottoming to a floor, eight feet across.

Quickly, before the clouds hugged all the way to the ground, the Eleans gathered what fallen branches they could find and started a fire to keep them warm and burn the dense vapor away from their hole. And as dusk deepened to full dark, the fire cleared the air four feet above their heads as they sat, all the way to the end of the floor of the hollow. There the dense vapor rolled down to the bottom of its banks, forming a thick wall of white on every side that prevented the Eleans from seeing more than a few feet beyond the hollow. The clouds had made a room around them.

Exhausted, too tired even to eat, warmed by the fire and bun-dled in their wool covers, heads growing heavier with every wave of sleep, they all began nodding off, and soon they were gone. Then, around five in the morning, young Aeneas woke, now sufficiently rested but famished and cold. The fire had dwindled and no longer gave off enough heat to make a difference. He could see Hipponax, who had caught a bad chill, shivering under his blanket. Now, driven by his mother's example of tireless care for the sick, intent on finding more kindling to keep Hipponax warm, Aeneas climbed up the bank of the hollow. Reaching the top, swallowed completely by the thick white, he dropped to all fours and crawled forty feet across the ground until he bumped up against the trunk of a tree — its fog-covered black-bark limbs full of bright-red leaves. There he found a branch on the ground, small enough to carry but big enough for the fire. Grabbing it, he stood up and turned to go back.

Suddenly, all around him, he heard frenzied sniffing, but he could not see anything through the thick white. His eyes and face transformed with fear as he realized that wild animals were just yards away—perhaps vicious boars with long tusks. He tried to

move, but his trembling legs would not. He tried to call for help, but no sound came out. Panic had taken hold. Then, from behind the tree, a large wolf (with shaggy, silver-gray fur and a huge head) sprang at his neck. Aeneas saw its snarling fangs, bared under its black muzzle, flying at him through the mist. He flinched. The wolf, its snapping jaws barely missing his throat, sailed on through, vanishing into the fog before it landed. Holding the branch out in front to ward his attacker off, Aeneas turned to face it. But before the same creature could come at him again, Aeneas, through the soft leather of his long boot, felt a sharp twinge at the back of his left calf. And then he felt a searing pain near the top of his right thigh.

Aeneas' screams woke his friends back at the camp. Immediately realizing that something was terribly wrong, they rose quickly and grabbed up their wooden staffs.

"Did you hear that?" Cadmus bleated. "Where's Aeneas?"

"Aeneas!" shouted Hipponax, into the fog. "Aeneas, can you hear us? Say something! Where are you?"

But Aeneas did not reply.

Now his three friends wrapped their wool caps on the ends of their staffs and stuck them into the few glowing embers that remained of the fire. It had not rained in the last two days, and so the cloths were dry enough to light. Then, waving the fiery ends of the staffs out in front, trying to clear the air, the three leapt up the bank of the hollow and started into the fog in the direction from which they all thought the screams had come.

"Aeneas," shouted Hipponax, desperately. "Aeneas, where are

you?" Then they waited a moment, but there was no answer.

Now sensing the worst and anxiously hoping for the best, the three, walking side-by-side, slowly pressed on through the trees, along the flat base of the gorge. And as they stumbled forward over the stony ground, not knowing what danger lurked in the fog, they kept calling for Aeneas, ever more panic in their voices.

Thirty yards further on, through the white, they began making out shadows stalking close, all around them, low to the ground. Instinctively, the three friends moved back to back to defend from every side against what they now realized from the growls (because they still could not see them clearly through the blanket) must be a large pack of ravenous mountain wolves.

"Stay calm," Hipponax reassured as the snarling circle of shadows walked in on them, now no more than six feet away. Then, without warning, the giant jabbed hard with the fiery end of his staff at one of the shadows standing right in front of him. He knew that whatever he hit was big and strong because the end of the staff that he was holding twisted in his palms from the impact. Yet, either from the force of the blow or because it had been burned, the creature let out a terrifying yelp and ran off howling, far into the fog, down the length of the echoing gorge.

Undaunted, the other wolves continued to walk slowly forward to within a few feet. Now the three friends could see the foaming muzzles and long teeth as the animals' faces came out of the vapor towards them.

Orion dipped to one knee; with both hands clasping tight to the other end of his staff, he quickly swept the fiery end out, from right to left in a wide arc, glancing a stern blow with the scorching tip across the snouts of four of the creatures. Like the first, they turned tail and ran off howling into the fog, along the canyon floor.

Cadmus, trying to copy Orion's move on his side of the advancing circle, dropped to one knee and swiftly slung a sweeping strike. It missed. But the end of the staff passed just close enough to the wolves for the fire to singe their noses.

Just as unexpectedly as the shadows had appeared, the remaining creatures all backed away and vanished into the mist. But the fire had consumed almost all the cloth that the Eleans had wrapped around their staffs. If they were to extinguish, the wolves would feel undeterred to resume their attack. So the three companions tore off pieces of their clothes to add to the ends of their staffs to keep the flames going, while they waited and watched to see if the wolves would advance on them again.

A few minutes passed without incident, though they all felt sick to their stomachs, from the fright and from the gnawing feeling that they were already too late to rescue Aeneas. Then, fully resolved to find him, they started walking forward again, not knowing where the creatures were, or if they would run into them.

For the rest of the night, they continued wandering around in the fog, doubling back many times over the same ground, adding cloth to the ends of their staffs as needed, calling for Aeneas, more alarm in their voices with each passing moment. Dawn came. Still they had not found him, and still the mist had not thinned to allow them to see any better.

Finally, around eight in the morning, the blanket began to lift back up to the branches in places, leaving dense patches surrounding pockets of perfectly clear air near the ground. About twenty minutes later, the three Eleans (in a moment of horror that none of them ever forgot) emerged from one of the white clumps into a large pocket of clear air. Aeneas was lying face-down on the ground, some ten feet in front of them, at the foot of the big, black tree, mist still swirling its cap of bright-red leaves.

"Aeneas!" shouted Orion, as he and the others ran towards the motionless, mangled body. Orion arrived first, went to his knees, and turned Aeneas over.

He was dead. But Orion's mind could not grasp it. "Aeneas," he pleaded, his voice overflowing with the deepest and most desperate of emotions. "Come on. Wake up. Just wake up. Please."

Cadmus, equally shaken but able to keep with reality, came up behind Orion and put his hand on his shoulder. "Orion, it's over. There's nothing we can do for him now."

Orion, tears flowing freely as he tried to come to terms with the fact that his cousin lay lifeless in front of him, plopped from his knees onto his seat.

Cadmus and Hipponax joined him on the ground around Aeneas. For a long while, they all just sat crying, too filled with grief to speak; but as it moved past midday into early afternoon, sometimes laughing through their sobs, they began remembering out loud all the best memories and times of Aeneas' life. Then the deep despair sank in on them again as they decided what they must do next. They could not stay any longer. They must get moving, or the wolves might come again that night to claim more victims. Now, once more too grieved for words, solemnly, they buried Aeneas in a shallow grave, next to the tree below which he had fallen. His staff and the clothes his mother had made for him would be his only company through eternity in this lonely place.

❧

The three remaining Eleans swept swiftly away from the gorge and never saw the wolves again. Over the next week, they continued across the mountains, deeply saddened but more determined than ever. Finally, on the far side of the range, among its high foothills, they found the road that wound down towards Corinth and the isthmus that would take them to Athens. To the left of the narrow gravel path, the grassy hillside rose steeply, three hundred feet above their heads. To the right, the ground fell away below the road, sharply down for a hundred green feet to a rocky base.

Four miles later, the Eleans approached a blind bend where the road wrapped around the green face to the left. Suddenly, when they reached within thirty yards of it, they heard the deep rumbling of horses coming fast towards them along the road ahead. Now the three travelers moved to the right edge of the gravel path, just before it joined the steep drop down. There they stood, waiting for the riders to appear and then pass. Soon the pounding hoofs and jangling harnesses were right around the corner. And then five mounted Spartans, one in the lead and two abreast after that, stormed into view; the Spartans were heading right at the Eleans, not slowing the mounts or directing them away from the three friends standing on the edge, even though the space was hardly wide enough for everyone. The Eleans would have to move or risk being trampled. But with nowhere to go, except tumbling down the steep drop below, they held fast, Hipponax at the front.

As the horses reached the three Eleans, those closest to the huge man flinched and veered into the others, almost throwing the riders as they sped by. But all the horsemen managed to stay up, even as their pace carried them past the Eleans, some thirty yards more, before they pulled to a stop in a cloud of dust.

Now the Eleans turned to face the five mounted soldiers (including vicious General Brasidas on the same white stallion with gray spots that he had ridden before the attack on Athens) coming slowly back towards them, an ominous sight. Long, plaited hair and short beards adorned the sinister faces under the bronze helmets with red crests. The armor clad bodies loomed aggressively atop the snorting mounts. Clearly, the Spartans, who held little regard for those not of their own kind and who thought nothing of meting out pain, were in little mood for pleasantries. His pride stinging from the failed siege of Athens, Brasidas had not marched back to Sparta with the rest of the army. Instead, he had (with these four attendants) visited the allied city of Thebes to ensure its support for the next season of fighting. Now he and his men were sweeping down past Corinth to Sparta in the south.

The Spartans reached Orion and his friends, standing at the side of the road, looking up at them.

"How dare you block our way," Brasidas scowled as his men

dismounted and came threateningly towards the Eleans.

"What are you talking about?" protested Cadmus, standing up to the menacing strangers. He never allowed himself to be bullied, an act in peaceful Elis that did not have the same serious consequences as here. "You almost ran us over."

"That's right," added Hipponax, puffing out his enormous barrel chest. "You don't own the road!"

"Kill them!" commanded the Spartan general from atop his horse, infuriated by what he regarded as insolent strangers whose lives were no more important than the lowly Helots he readily butchered back in Sparta.

Instantly, Hipponax's massive fists felled the soldier standing in front of him before the soldier could draw his sword.

Orion also acted too quickly for the Spartan standing nearest him, whipping his staff from his back and cracking his attacker on the thigh (right above the protected kneecap) to drop him to the ground holding his leg. Brasidas, having dismounted to join the fight, sword drawn, rushed right in on Orion. But the Elean dodged the Spartan general's vicious lunges until eventually he stepped to the left and struck with his wood across the side of his attacker's neck. Brasidas wobbled forward. Then he slumped down unconscious at the right edge of the road, next to the start of the sharp, green drop down.

Now Orion, his own assailants disabled, looked for his friends. Both of them, having somehow lost their staffs to the ground, were in dire straits. Hipponax was anxiously backing against the cliff wall on the left of the road, a sword pointed right at him by an expres-

sionless Spartan. Puny Cadmus (acrobatically darting and ducking
to evade his pursuer's slashing blade) was running around the blind
corner on the road ahead, in a desperate attempt to shake his
attacker off.

The first Spartan drew back his sword to plunge it into Hipponax; but Orion, reaching at the last possible moment to save his
friend, smashed his staff against the side of the soldier's neck, knocking him out. Like a stone, the Spartan fell straight to the gravel.

"Thanks, Orion," Hipponax nodded quickly as he bent down
to recover his staff from the ground.

"Cadmus," shouted Orion, as he and Hipponax raced towards
the bend, not knowing what was happening to him on the other
side of it.

Cadmus, still dodging his attacker's vicious swipes, was relieved
to hear Orion calling him, and he bolted for the safety of his
friends, the Spartan in hot pursuit.

Cadmus, small and speedy, made it around the corner in time.
But he tripped and fell at Hipponax's feet as he did, and then the
Spartan emerged, sword raised to strike. But before the Spartan
could reach close enough for his swing to count, Hipponax jabbed
his staff straight out into the advancing soldier's throat, knocking
him onto his back holding his neck.

"You okay?" Orion asked as Hipponax pulled Cadmus to his
feet.

"I'm fine," Cadmus replied, looking around at the enemy, very
impressed with his friends. The assailants were all down in various
states of disrepair, three blacked out and two rolling around in

agony. "And you?"

"We're fine," replied Orion. "But let's hurry up and get out of here." The Eleans had no desire to harm their assailants further. They just wanted to go peacefully. And if the Spartans recovered, they would surely fight again, and then it could easily go the other way. The first time, the killing machines, not having expected the simply dressed Eleans to respond so assertively or to put up such a good fight, had been caught off guard and had not been at their best. That would not happen a second time, and so now the Eleans scrambled around gathering their own fallen belongings from the ground—the leather water pouches, food boxes, and blanket rolls that Hipponax and Cadmus had flung at the enemy in desperate attempts to slow their attackers.

Then Cadmus approached General Brasidas to claim the sword resting next to him, and Hipponax took the blade by which he had almost died two minutes before. They would keep these weapons in case anyone else attacked them on the road.

Orion refused to gather a sword. As herald of the Olympic Truce, he would not take up a weapon of war. But he did help himself to better transportation. He, Cadmus, and Hipponax each jumped on one of the horses; and they also grabbed the reins of the two remaining steeds to trail them along behind. Then the Eleans rode away, quickly disappearing around the bend in the road ahead, leaving their attackers strewn across the gravel behind.

Now the three friends were traveling in style.

Chapter Five

ATHENS

Days later, the three Eleans rode south over the gentle coastal mountains that separated Athens from the broad Attica plain, and the city came into view. Their destination was widely known as the commercial and cultural center of the entire Greek world. They had expected it would be impressive. But still Orion and his friends were taken aback by the magnificence of the sight that now lay below the last of the range, and they stared in wonder, eyes wide and jaws dropped open, not a word between them, taking it all in.

Directly ahead of the Eleans, seven hundred yards further in the distance, across the flat, open, shrubby ground of the narrow coastal strip of land, lay the Dipylon and Sacred Gateways. Athens' tall perimeter wall wrapped around the entire city and stretched, in a narrow corridor at its southwest edge, all the way down to the bustling port, four miles away, its three harbors packed with merchant ships. Inside Athens, houses for its ninety thousand citizens, made of white-plastered mud bricks and sloping clay-tile roofs, occupied every available space not used for a public purpose, right up to within a few feet of the city wall in many places. Narrow, winding, paved streets ran between the houses, which had sprouted without much planning. But most of them, mansions to more humble homes, followed the same general design, built around a central courtyard with the wooden front door of the house abutting the path coursing between it and its neighbors. There was only one very broad road in Athens, the Panathenaic Way. Its paved length ran directly from the Dipylon Gateway to the mouth of the Agora. There it bent to the right and went straight through the teeming marketplace. Then it continued on to the stone steps that led up the massive limestone hill atop which the Acropolis sat. The walled sanctuary that dominated Athens' skyline originally was a fort. But now it was filled with rectangular white-marble temples, including the gigantic Parthenon, dedicated to Athena.

The Eleans, now walking and leading the five horses by the reins, entered the Dipylon Courtyard. Its ramparts were manned atop by a thousand soldiers, and the ground in front of its two closed doors was guarded by thirty soldiers: Athenians, Scythians, and Plataeans.

As the Eleans continued along, they could not help but look up at the thousand sentries above and at the thirty ahead, wondering what they would do. Then the Eleans reached the contingent outside the two oak doors and halted.

"Welcome, strangers," said Euripedes, fifty-year-old Athenian army captain. The stern ranking officer on the ground in front of the portals was a tall, broad-shouldered, balding man with sullen features. "Everyone may enter Athens who comes in peace."

"We come in peace," replied Orion.

"Then surrender your weapons and enter," commanded the captain.

Five men with mustard scorpions on their shields stepped assertively forward towards the Eleans, and the three friends willingly handed over their wooden staffs and the two swords taken from the Spartans on the road.

"Open!" Euripedes shouted as he and his men stepped out of the way to let the Eleans through. The left door swung open quickly and then closed hard behind them as they passed inside the city and started down the Panathenaic Way, heading towards the mouth of the Agora.

Now the Plataean guard holding the two swords given to him by Cadmus and Hipponax noticed that they were of Spartan make. Concerned, he showed the blades to Euripedes, who eyed them closely. Drawing the same conclusion, the broad-shouldered captain commanded the portal open again and then, just as it swung ajar, turned to his men, focusing on a trio of Scythians standing nearest him. "You three—come with me!"

Accompanied by the trio of deadly archers, he passed into the city after the Eleans, keeping his distance behind so as not to be seen, while he watched the strangers to discover their intentions. Euripedes wanted to confront them, but he did not yet have enough proof that they intended harm, and he was afraid of being punished again by Athens' leaders. The captain, contrary to the ruling council, favored closing the city to all outsiders as a means to counteract Spartan spying, and he had in the past been severely censured and even demoted for taking far too heavy a hand with innocent suspects.

The three from Elis, leading the five horses by the reins, walked on deeper down the broad Panathenaic Way, crowded with people doing business in the houses of the skilled craftsmen lining it on both sides. Fascinated by everything around, Orion and his friends did not realize that sentries were tracing their every step.

"Just when you think it can't get any better, then here we are!" exclaimed Cadmus, eyes big with delight as he and the others reached the Agora, Athens' bustling hub of activity.

At the center of the marketplace, directly ahead of them—parted down its middle by the Panathenaic Way running through its entire length—was a large open area. It was packed with goods-laden market stalls, containing every imaginable commodity. And it was crowded with merchants, customers, foreign traders, and market officials.

The covered colonnades around the edges of the crowded open area housed the shops of the finest craftsmen and the offices of lawyers, bankers, and doctors. Public buildings were interspersed with the colonnades at the Agora's edge: the Law Courts, Prison, Council Buildings, and Fountain House—where women came every morning to exchange news and gather the fresh water spewing out of the four stone lion heads.

"They have everything here, and look at the food," Cadmus blurted as the three Eleans, walking along the left edge of the Panathenaic Way, entered the vibrant market. They were distracted in every direction by the lively activity, even as they reached halfway down its length.

Then, suddenly, through the crowd, Orion spotted Aria, a young woman of his age. She was walking towards him, some hundred feet away, between the stalls on the other side of the road. Long, light-brown hair flowed like shining silk down on both sides of her oval face to frame her tanned, angular features; chestnut-colored, almond-shaped eyes; and perfect, soft lips. Her long legs and tall, slender body were apparent even under her white, ankle-length tunic with yellow trim.

Orion noticed the taller and far more robust young woman forcefully striding along next to Aria, talking her ear off while Aria listened patiently. Medea, Aria's homely sister (with more exaggerated features) was a year younger than Aria.

Quickly Orion's eyes, drawn by the raw force of instinct, swept back to beauty. He could not keep from staring at her even if he wanted to (which he did not). She was the ideal he had always imagined but had never found. It was as if the gods had entered the core of his deepest desires to craft her in the exact image that stirred his most powerful passions.

As Aria drew to the edge of the Panathenaic Way—though still on the other side of the road from him—she realized that Orion was gawking at her. She boldly locked eyes with him, yoked with equal force by her attraction to him. Then, glancing away, she tried to conceal it. Orion continued staring directly at her, not paying attention to where he was going until, still transfixed, he accidentally guided one of his trailing horses right into a cloth merchant's stall, plowing it over on top of the merchant. Pytheas fell to the ground as the stall's poles, cloth roof, and the yards of colorful fabric, which had been so elegantly displayed on a wooden rack above his head, came down on him with it.

Orion immediately ran over and began pulling the debris off the fifty-five-year-old merchant, still flailing around underneath, trying to extricate himself. Orion uncovered a head of thinning, brown hair. And then he found a stubby arm, by which he hoisted up the short and round old man with jolly face.

"Are you alright?" asked Orion, concerned. "I'm so sorry."

"Yes, I'm fine," replied the curious merchant. He was far from angry, even though he might easily have been, under the circumstances. "But what happened? One minute I was standing there, and the next thing I know, I was buried under a sea of fabric."

"Well, there was..." said Orion, embarrassed at the disaster he had caused as he began explaining the reason for it.

"Father, are you alright?" interrupted Aria, who had run up behind Orion.

"Yes, my dear," Pytheas replied warmly. "All is well. No broken bones." He paused for a second, and then an enormous smile burst onto his kindly face. Orion and Aria were once more spellbound in each other's presence. Pytheas had never seen his elder daughter show the least bit of interest in any of the many suitors who had knocked on his door trying to win her. But now her attraction to this handsome stranger was unmistakable, as was his to her.

What Pytheas did not notice was that his sturdy younger daughter, Medea, had come up behind Cadmus (whom she towered over) and tapped him on the shoulder. Much to Cadmus' horror, he turned around to find her smiling at him. Her close physical resemblance to Herpylla, his unwelcome suitor back in Elis, startled him a great deal and troubled him even more. He moved away from her. But, annoying him, she followed, keeping close.

"Sir, I did knock your stall over," said Orion, respectfully continuing his conversation with brimming Pytheas. "I would be happy to pay for any damages."

Medea winked at Cadmus, which only infuriated him. However, Hipponax, who had been observing their game of cat and mouse from the moment that Medea approached behind Cadmus, was most amused by his friend's predicament, especially when Medea continued to nudge closer to fleeing Cadmus.

"You are an honorable young man," Pytheas said to Orion. "Where are you from? Your accent is not like any I ever heard."

"My friends and I have traveled from Elis, two hundred miles to the west," Orion replied.

"What brings you such a long way?" Pytheas inquired with the same growing curiosity reflected on Aria's face. "Do you come to Athens to sell or to buy?"

"Neither," said Orion. "We have come to deliver a great message of peace to your leaders."

"Our city is governed by the Athenian Council," Aria answered warmly, intending to be as helpful as she could. "We the people of

Athens elect them to rule for our benefit."

"And how may I gain an audience with this Athenian Council?" asked Orion, somewhat worried that they would pose an obstacle similar to the obstinate Hellanodikes. "Is it difficult?"

"Quite the opposite," reassured Pytheas, having heard the doubt in Orion's voice. "Every day before lunch the council considers petitions from anyone who wishes to address it. If you hurry, you can have yours heard today."

"They meet over there, in the Council Chamber," added Aria, pointing across the Agora to a large, rectangular white-plaster hall, sitting with other buildings inside a walled courtyard on the market's northwest corner. A gaping doorway in the high enclosing wall, guarded outside by ten Scythians, led into the courtyard.

"First let me help you restore your things to their proper place," said Orion, gratefully addressing Pytheas. "And then we can decide if I owe anything for the damages."

"No," Pytheas responded. "You have important business. You run along now. Just be sure to come back when you're done, and we'll settle everything over a hot meal."

"Thank you," Orion replied. "We'll be back as soon as we can." He nodded to Aria, and she returned a smile. Then he turned to his friends. "Let's go."

"See you later," Medea said to Cadmus, annoying him even more as he left.

The three Eleans walked away through the market, Hipponax teasing Cadmus about Medea every step of the way until they reached the ten Scythians standing outside the entrance in the courtyard's enclosing wall. The guards searched them, took their horses, and let them through the doorway to join the back of the line of people in the courtyard that led up to the Council Chamber's bronze-plated double door, set flush in its white-plaster front wall.

A scribe, who took himself far too seriously, walked forward from in front of the door to attend to them. "Name?" he demanded.

"Orion of Elis," Orion replied, politely offering a smile. "I am here to ask the great men of the…"

"Save it for inside," snapped the scribe, cutting him off. "You will be heard in about an hour. Be quiet and wait your turn."

After twice that long, just before noon, the last person in front of them in the line emerged from inside the chamber, happier than he had entered. Then the scribe let the three Eleans pass in, shutting the door behind.

The twenty-foot-wide green-marble debate floor occupied the middle of the room for the entire length under the high ceiling. The hall's walls were all painted, in full color, with life-sized scenes depicting heroes and gods. Down each side of the debate floor, backed by the long walls of both sides of the hall, ran five terraced rows of wooden benches; they were filled with five hundred council members, important-looking men of all physical descriptions, young and old, all very serious.

Cleon, a stately older man, about sixty, got up from his seat in the middle of the front row of the right-side benches, walked to the center of the debate floor, and motioned to the three Eleans.

"Please come forward to state your petition." When Pericles was alive, Cleon clashed with him over war strategy. After Pericles' death, Cleon, relying on strong support from the Athenian common man, replaced him as Speaker of Athens' ruling body. And it did not surprise anyone that Cleon, then the most powerful political figure, immediately used his position to support General Demosthenes' more aggressive deployments. Yet, even after General Nicias won a return to the more defensive strategy, the council retained Cleon as Speaker because of his steadfast adherence to the democratic principles upon which it was based, not to mention his considerable skill at administering the council's lively debates.

Orion, followed by Hipponax and Cadmus, joined Cleon. Then Orion delivered the message from Zeus, explaining that he did not need the blessing of the Hellanodikes because Zeus had spoken to him directly.

When Orion was done, twenty-eight-year-old Colonel Alcibiades (the most glamorous and handsome man in all Athens) rose from his seat in the gallery. Pericles, his mother's brother, had raised Alcibiades from just three years old, after Alcibiades' father had died. Having been groomed for greatness (it was expected of him, and he expected it of himself), he often tried to direct attention his way, sometimes by deriding others. "And how exactly did Zeus transmit his will to you?"

"He came to me in a vision," responded Orion, in all sincerity, "in the middle of the night, after I fell asleep."

Complete silence.

Then, as one, the entire Athenian Council broke into uproarious laughter. Alcibiades, self-satisfied, sat.

"You almost had us," Cleon chuckled. "Who put you up to this? Was it Aristophanes?" The dramatist known for his comedies also was notorious for attempting practical jokes on a grand scale.

"Nobody put me up to this," replied Orion, frustrated for being laughed at as if he were a clowning idiot. "This is the word of Zeus. You must make them listen. All of Greece depends on this."

Orion's reply was certain and serious enough to convey to Cleon that he may well have been sincere.

"Are you sure this is not some kind of prank?" asked Cleon.

"I assure you," answered Orion, solemnly, "this is no game. Zeus has ordered me to do this."

"Alright," Cleon shrugged, clearly still skeptical but intent on fulfilling his role as Speaker. "Have it your way. But be warned, the council members can strip the flesh from your bones with their sharp tongues, especially on matters as important as this."

Cleon turned his attention to the galleries on both sides, still in an uproar. Some of the council members were standing in the aisles, and others were almost falling out of their seats because they were laughing so hard.

"Esteemed Members, come to order please," Cleon shouted as he motioned with his hands for the galleries to quiet. Respectfully, they took their seats and silenced. "This matter is indeed *unusual*, to say the least, but this young man, for reasons that we will soon discover, insists that he be heard. So now, we are bound by the rules of our great council to give his petition full and fair consideration."

Again Alcibiades rose from his seat, sarcasm dripping from his every word. "Then I shall begin the debate by saying that I fully and fairly consider him a lunatic."

Again, to the great discomfort of Orion and his friends, the gallery erupted, delighted by Alcibiades' humor. For a full minute, Alcibiades stood pompously, looking around with his arms open and a smile on his face, accepting their applause and cheers.

The council calmed as cautious General Nicias rose from his seat, obviously intending to add his judgment. "And I say he is a swindler of some sort, who has concocted this wild scheme for his own advantage. Imagine how wealthy a man could become if everyone believed that he speaks for Zeus. There would be no end to contributions from those seeking the gods' favor. And as for his influence, well, that would know no bounds."

The whole council pondered Nicias' suggestion. Orion folded his arms, feeling very uncomfortable as he realized that their decision was now entirely beyond his control. Saying anything else would only serve to alienate the gallery further. Arguing with the Hellanodikes had done no good and had put them more against him, a result he did not wish to repeat here.

Bearded Socrates, forty-two, his lack of grooming and large facial features offending all sense of style and proportion, rose somewhat pretentiously from his seat in the gallery. The finest scholar in Athens was a far keener evaluator of facts than Alcibiades, his pupil who showed great potential but had much to learn. And now Socrates took a more "erudite" tack in assessing Orion. "This young man is neither a lunatic nor a swindler. He is just a naïve country dweller who is without education. Guided more by superstition than by reason, as befitting his regrettable condition, he has believed his own dream to be real. He is nothing more and nothing less than a misguided simpleton who, I am willing to wager, has never been mistaken for a man of learning even in his own home."

The council, swayed by his status as the greatest thinker of their day, nodded their heads in agreement. Then Socrates, knowing that now their ears were willing, continued. "However, that being said, perhaps there is some merit to the idea of reviving the Olympic Games as a means to achieve peace with Sparta. The games did indeed work well for other warring nations to accomplish similar ends in times past. Might we not consider them for the same purpose again?"

All of a sudden, Euripedes, guard captain from the city gate, accompanied by the three Scythian archers, stormed out to the center of the debate floor from the shadows of the entryway, where they had been secretly waiting. He and his men had followed the three Eleans all the way to the Council Chamber and slipped quietly inside the door when Orion began delivering his message. They had heard every word of the discussion.

"These men are spies, sent here to lure us into a trap," Euripedes declared sternly, raising high the two swords taken from Hipponax and Cadmus, one in each hand. "See these Spartan blades. They belong to them. And their horses, tethered outside, bear a striking resemblance to the type bred in Sparta."

Everyone stared hard at the three Eleans, deeply suspicious.

This explanation could more reasonably account for Orion's suppli-
cation than his extraordinary claims.

"Can you resolve this?" Cleon asked, turning to Orion. "How
do you come to carry these weapons and to ride such stallions?"

"We were attacked by five soldiers in the mountains west of
Corinth," Cadmus, coming to Orion's aid, proclaimed to the whole
room.

"That's right," added Hipponax, quite proud. "My friends and
I trounced them and took their swords and their horses. And that's
how we have them."

The council members looked at the Eleans with even greater
suspicion than before. Their explanation was too far-fetched to be
real.

"They are lying!" shouted Nicias, jumping to his feet. "Death to
the Spartan spies! Hang them!"

Euripides, Spartan swords pointed, and the three Scythians,
bows loaded and arrows aimed, moved purposefully towards Orion
and his friends.

General Demosthenes, the ruggedly handsome savior of Athens, rose serenely from his seat in the gallery. "Leave them be," he
commanded in his strong, calm, confident voice.

Euripides and the sentries immediately stopped their advance.

"Spartan spies would not be so foolish as to carry Spartan
swords and ride Spartan horses," continued Demosthenes. "They
may be lying, but spies they are not."

Demosthenes paused for a moment as the council warmed to
his reasoning. Then he continued. "If these men do indeed convey

a message from Zeus, then it is at our peril that we ignore them and the promise of peace that the Olympic Games hold. On the other hand, we must be sure they really do bear divine blessing. Otherwise, we could never trust the Spartans to keep the truce, without the gods to ensure their compliance."

"What exactly are you proposing?" asked Cleon, as confused as the rest of the council.

"Let us test them," said Demosthenes.

"And how should we do that?" inquired Cleon, voicing everyone's growing curiosity.

"We will send them on a quest that no one could accomplish unless they were guided by the hand of Zeus. If they complete it, then Athens will agree to participate in the Olympic Games."

"What do you all say to this?" Cleon asked the council.

Socrates stood again. "Demosthenes has soundly postulated the problem. Does his solution not seem the most logical since it accounts for both sides of the coin?"

"Does everyone agree?" Cleon asked, and the council assented, some reluctantly. Nicias and Alcibiades, especially, would have preferred a different outcome, the former because he disagreed and the latter because he was jealous of Demosthenes.

But Demosthenes' argument, backed by Socrates, already had won most hearts and minds. And both Nicias and Alcibiades, preserving credibility for future debates, chose to cede rather than proffer a losing proposition.

Cleon turned to Orion. "Do you accept this charge?"

"I do," Orion replied confidently, realizing he had no other choice. Cadmus and Hipponax stood with their arms folded, less than pleased that their journey had become more complicated still.

Cleon turned to Demosthenes again. "Do you have a task in mind?"

Demosthenes nodded and then turned to the Eleans. "Do you know who the Amazons are?"

"Not really," replied Orion. "We have heard of them in stories, but we did not know they still walk the earth." The faded race, while having occupied the entire Greek imagination in previous centuries, no longer garnered much attention on the mainland since now they mostly troubled other places across the known world.

"They are a tribe of fierce women warriors who carry shields shaped like a half moon and wear clothes made from the skins of wild animals," explained Demosthenes. "They live on an island far off our coast, but they venture from it to raid foreign shores for spoils and for other things."

Demosthenes, shaking his head regretfully, paused a moment. Then he continued, more somber now. "On a summer night, some fifteen years ago, their ships slipped secretly onto a beach near Athens. Undetected, using vines as ropes, they stole over the walls and into the city. Through an open window, they entered the house of our finest musician, Callinus, and took his daughter, Carina, just four years old, from her bed, while he and his wife slept. Two Athenian sentries spotted the Amazon warriors as they streamed back over the walls to leave. The guards raised the alarm. Then, realizing that time was short, they gave chase before reinforcements could arrive. Amazon arrows quickly felled those two brave men. Then the fierce women warriors escaped in their boats before more Athenian guards could reach. We sent our own vessels after them, but our ships were too big to catch their smaller and more manageable craft, which easily darted away from us at sharp angles, disappearing into the night across the calm water before we could turn to follow."

Demosthenes paused again, the weight of his memory seeming to grow even heavier. Then, with another sigh, he continued. "Intent on rescuing Carina, we sailed all the way to the Amazons' home. But it did not go well. Beyond its sandy beaches, their entire island is covered by a thick jungle, in which the savage women waited for us, well hidden. And as we entered it, we became easy targets for the spears and arrows flying at us through the leaves. We never even saw where they came from or who had dispatched them. Still, despite heavy losses, determined to rescue the innocent young girl, our soldiers (most had left Athens too quickly to gather their armor) pressed on deeper into the jungle. We were heading towards the center of the island, where the Amazons' stone palace is reputed to sit. And as we drew closer to it, the savages' attack became more desperate and wild. Now, one by one, with ear-piercing shrieks, they jumped out from behind the bushes as we passed, striking deadly blows with their axes and swords, then quickly retreating back into hiding, behind the leaves, before we could respond. We were being attacked from all sides and did not know from where the next one would come. The toll was terrible and terrifying, and we would all have been killed if those of us remaining had not run for the safety of our ships, carrying the injured on our backs. The pack of Amazons, still hidden behind the vegetation, followed, brutally culling our number as we retreated, their collective shrieks so shrill and frenzied that they radiated down our spines. By the time we arrived on the shore, we had lost nine out of every ten men who had braved the jungle."

Demosthenes, regret mixed with sorrow written all over his face, paused again.

"Do you know what happened to Carina?" asked Orion, with genuine empathy for the loss of life and deeply concerned for the plight of the defenseless young girl.

"We are not sure," Demosthenes replied. "That is why you must travel to the island of the Amazons to see if you can retrieve her. We will provide you with a ship and enough gold and silver for a ransom."

"I gladly accept," Orion replied. "We will do everything we can to bring her home."

Demosthenes nodded, appreciative yet solemn. He admired Orion's courage in being so willing to rescue Athens' treasured daughter. But he wondered if the young stranger had not undertaken a task that was indeed impossible, even with help from Olympus. Carina could well be dead, and if she was still alive, the Amazons would have bent her to their ways and made the kidnapped young girl one of them, an art in which they were well practiced as a primary means of adding to their tribe. Now that she was a member of their sisterhood, a warrior, they would hardly part with her. And even if Orion was somehow able to persuade the

Amazon queen to let the girl return to Athens, Carina herself probably would not want to, having by now joined in spirit with the feral females.

Chapter Six

AMAZONS

True to his word, Demosthenes provided the three Eleans with a sturdy timber merchant ship. Its sixty-foot-long hull was filled with large sacks containing coins, some of gold and others of silver, all stamped with the symbol of an owl.

The next day, the wind caught in the square canvas sail (it was white with a blue dolphin painted across it) flying on the vessel's single mast, and the three friends sailed out of Athens' port, waving to the crowd gathered on the shore. Hipponax stood steering at the back. Orion and Cadmus stood at the narrowed prow, above the large eyes painted on the outside of its both sides to ward off evil.

Piraeus became a dot far behind and then vanished as the Eleans headed south and rounded the lowest tip of Attica. Now they sailed northeast up the Aegean. Never buffeted by the storms that often tormented mariners at this time of year, each day the Eleans glided a mile for every foot that their vessel was long, and soon they reached and passed through the narrow strait leading into the Black Sea. Then they went straight across (in the same line as they had entered) to three-quarters of the ocean's length.

The island of the Amazons was close (according to what Demosthenes had told them), and now the Eleans began thinking more intensely about what else Demosthenes had recounted about the Amazons, all that he could surmise. At the beginning of all memory, they were an exclusively female tribe of hard-riding horsewomen that inhabited the wild lands around the River Tanais, east of the Black Sea. Over the course of time, their warriors fought and defeated all other tribes in the untamed territory, adding the women to their own clan and mating with and then killing the men. The resulting female offspring were raised as one of them, but all male babies were discarded to the elements to die. Then three and a half centuries ago, around the time that the Olympic Games were first held, the growing number of Amazons began roaming far beyond their homeland, seeking out more men to put deep under their heels. Now their mounted packs knifed into Asia Minor and Greece. Once, their whole army, at the zenith of their power, came all the way to Athens. But the Athenian infantry charged outside the city walls and broke through the right wing of their cavalry line and then wheeled behind its center and other flank to inflict heavy losses. That battle forced the Amazons to withdraw from Greece. It also caused their decline. A fact never lost on them. Soon, depleted, they suffered other crushing defeats and were driven out of

Asia Minor by an alliance of barbarian hordes. Fearful that they would be hunted on the open grasslands of the wild territory, the few hundred remaining Amazons freed their horses to roam the plains and left their accustomed home to take refuge far from it on the easily defended island where their descendants still live.

"There it is!" shouted Cadmus, standing at the prow as the Amazons' home came into view amid the shimmering water half-way between the Eleans and the horizon. Hipponax, his back drenched by sunset, still in charge of the rudder at the stern, steered directly for it.

Swept along by ample winds, the Eleans' ship drew to within fifty yards of the wide, sandy beach. Beyond it, the round island, nine miles to the center from any point on the shore, was over-grown with thick, green foliage. Tall trees (with straight trunks, cauliflower-shaped leaf-tops, and long vines hanging down) towered above the dense growth of big-leafed plants that was packed tight near the damp ground around their mangles of massive buttress roots.

The Eleans dropped the sail and sent the anchor through the shallow water to the sandy bottom. But they did not go to land. Instead, the three companions remained onboard, crouched behind the safety of the ship's waist-high walls, leaving only their heads exposed to anyone who might be watching from inside the jungle, while they waited for the Amazons to reveal themselves. The beach may have been empty, but the Eleans could feel the wild, unfriend-ly eyes fixed on them from inside the dense vegetation.

Three hours later, after the sun had disappeared, a party of two hundred women (tall, athletic warriors, scantily clad in animal skins) emerged from the jungle onto the shore, under the light of the bright, star-filled sky. They were heavily armed with an assortment of weapons: bows (ready to sling bronze-tipped arrows), spears, axes, and swords (rounded broad on both sides to match the shape of the long leaves in their island home).

"What are you doing here?" screamed Antiope, the forty-year-old Amazon queen, dressed in leopard. She had long, fire-red, braided hair and a harsh, rasping voice that matched the bitter expression on her face, made hideous by a patchwork of battle scars. "No Athenian is welcome on this island." She had recognized the ship's origin by the distinctive eyes painted on the front of its hull; but it was manned by so few men that it did not pose a threat. And Antiope intended to keep its crew occupied long enough for the nimble Amazon war craft to speed from the other side of the island, where they were docked. Then her warriors could board the Athenian vessel before it had a chance to sail.

"We are not Athenians," replied Orion, remaining behind cover. The bronze-tipped Amazon shafts could easily reach the Athenian ship. "But we have been sent by them to secure release of their daughter, Carina. We bring a ransom of gold and silver."

"So they are too cowardly to do their own dirty work," snarled Antiope with disdain. "She belongs to us now. We paid a high price for her that no amount of gold or silver could repay." She rubbed her most disfiguring scar, coursing deeply down the entire center of her face from forehead to chin, not even skipping her lips. Demosthenes, with a frenzied downward swipe of his sword, had given it to her as she lunged at him from behind the thick foliage of the Amazon jungle, during the ill-fated attempt to rescue Carina, fifteen years previous. And it was during that same fierce struggle that the Athenian general, unknown to him, also had mortally wounded the then-queen, Lysippe, with a blind lunge through the nearby leaves that pierced her jugular. She bled to death on the jungle floor, cradled by her daughter, the present queen, in her arms.

From the unyielding determination in Antiope's tone, Orion realized that he must do something drastic if he was to have any hope of changing her mind. Desperate to plead his case and hoping to win her trust, he stood up straight, exposing his upper body to view, now an easy target for the skilled female archers on the shore. But Antiope did not order them to fire, which she might have done had the sight of Orion's muscular frame not overcome her to the extent that it did. In a single instant, she had been fully invaded by a desire that now, for the moment, consumed everything else, even hate.

"I beg you to reconsider," Orion pleaded, not having yet recognized his new-found favor. "Far more than one girl's fate rests on your decision. If you could just…"

"You must be tired after such a long journey," interrupted Antiope. "Surely you need something to restore your energies. Dine with me tonight, and I will consider your request. Your *sincerity* has won me."

Cadmus and Hipponax exchanged a smile, knowing full well why Antiope had suddenly changed her position. This was not the first time they had seen a woman succumb to handsome Orion's allure. And it seemed to have happened just in time. Five Amazon craft had arrived from the other side of the island. The thirty-foot-long, open-hulled vessels were powered by ten oars on both sides (in addition to the sail hanging from the single mast at mid-ship), and each carried twenty fully armed savage females, ready to board the visitors' ship.

"Done," said Orion, eager to press his advantage. "We will dine with you tonight."

"Then leave your weapons on your vessel," warned Antiope, "and come to shore."

Orion, Hipponax, and Cadmus, complying with the queen's demands, climbed over the side of their ship onto one of the Amazon craft—in among the women speaking excitedly in a strange, shrill tongue, while they prodded and poked the captives. Now the Amazons tethered the Eleans' hands with coarse vines, as thick and strong as the best rope. And accompanied by the other boats, they rowed the prisoners to shore to meet the rest of the tribe, waiting on the sand.

When the prows reached within ten feet of the beach, the warriors in each boat dropped their oars and jumped out into the waist-high water. They hauled the vessels the rest of the way, parking the front portions of their lengths on the sand and leaving their sterns in the shallows. Now they heaved the Eleans onto the land, and instantly, chattering in their shrill tongue, the whole pack surged around to inspect them.

Then, without warning, Antiope howled at the sky-full of stars,

and the Amazons, stopping their grating babble, swept silently into the jungle, leading their prisoners. There was no clear path over the slippery, damp ground. So, as they walked along, they brushed through dense banks of leaves and branches and skirted around the massive buttress roots of vine-draped tree trunks.

Two hours later, they suddenly came out of the bushes into a grass clearing. In the middle of it sat the Amazon Palace, a gigantic stone pyramid. Its peak was shaved off sixty feet before its sides would have risen to join in a point. Therefore, instead of a point, it showed a flat top. Square windows, open to the elements, were cut out of the pyramid's outer walls, and a rectangular stone archway led in.

Soon Orion found himself in Antiope's private dining quarters. The square room (with angled ceiling, deep-purple-painted walls, and soft-pink marble floor) was bathed in starlight through the window. At the center of the room, four wooden couches (with leopard-pelt cushions and blankets) were arranged around a low table, where the food rested within relatively easy reach. Roasted oysters on a plate and an overflowing bowl of green grapes.

For the moment, the hideous queen, who did nothing to mask her intentions, sat on the couch to the right of the one occupied by Orion. Meanwhile, the only other person in the room (a tall, blonde young woman) filled their earthen cups with wine from an ornately painted jug. Dressed in brown leather, she was obviously a new recruit, not yet fashioned to savage. Her round face, gentle eyes, and soft yet pleasing body were clearly different from the wild, hungry looks and lean-muscled frames of the warriors. Antiope, afraid that Orion would be more drawn to one of the more attractive and athletic women than herself, had ordered everyone besides this servant to retire with Hipponax and Cadmus to dine in the main hall.

The servant girl finished pouring the wine and started towards the doorway. Antiope got up from her seat and came over to sit next to Orion on the same couch. She took out her dagger and cut his bonds. Then she began passing her fingers gently over his wrists to soothe where the vines had scuffed them. But Orion, pretending to want a grape from the other side of the table, escaped to a different sofa, while he pried for information. "Which one is she? Is she the ugly one with the axe?"

The gigantic main dining hall occupied the entire center of the palace. The square room was free to the heavens through the top of the pyramid. And the hole to the sky sat far above the equally sized and shaped pool where fresh rainwater collected in the middle of the hall's pink marble floor. Around the pool, all the way back to the hall's walls, painted pale-green, the hall was furnished with a series of couches and tables, similar in design and arrangement to the queen's room.

Several hundred Amazons, who had not enjoyed the company of men in a long time, competed fiercely amongst themselves for the attention of the two already-untied Eleans. Hipponax would have nothing of it. Sitting on a couch in the corner, interested only in the food and wine, he was brushing aside the Amazons' advances with swipes of his enormous arms, often sending them tumbling away from him. Puny Cadmus wanted every part of it, and he sat on one of the couches right next to the pool, fully enjoying the avid attention being heaped on him by so many beautiful and athletic women of every description.

"Have some, Cadmus," offered Penthesilea, holding out a bunch of succulent grapes as she sat down next to him on the same couch. The alluring warrior looked and moved like the panther whose pelt she wore. The twenty-five-year-old had olive skin; a broad, catlike face; deep-yellow, passionate eyes; full lips; and long, black, flowing, kinky hair. Her lanky, six-foot-tall, 165-pound body was thin over the waist and ribs. But then it suddenly burst into long, lean, supple muscle at the buttocks and shoulders.

"Why have grapes when you can have wine?" protested Hippolyta, aggressively sweeping Penthesilea's offering out of the way to put a silver goblet to Cadmus' lips as she sat down on the same couch, on the other side of him. Hippolyta, born hours after Penthesilea, had a body, dressed in lion, almost identical to her bitter rival's, though she was not quite as tall. Her hair was blonde and straight and her face more long than wide and feline. But her blue eyes, golden-tanned skin, and softer but fuller lips were equally sultry in their own way. In addition to beauty, the two had competed in everything from the day they came into the world, including many bloody hand-to-hand battles as teenagers that the queen had since prohibited for fear of losing one of her fiercest fighters.

"Maybe he doesn't want wine, Hippolyta," snapped Penthesilea, glaring threateningly at her challenger.

"Why don't you just leave us alone?" responded Hippolyta,

raising the stakes. "He obviously likes me better."

"Come now, ladies," said Cadmus, completely full of himself.
"There's no need to fight. Haven't you heard of sharing?"

Cadmus took a sip of the wine. Penthesilea seethed at her rival.

Back in her private den, hideous Antiope, despite feeling the
influence of the wine far more than usual, had followed Orion to
the other couch and was about to force a kiss. But, suddenly, her
head felt too heavy to keep up, and she put it down in Orion's lap
and started snoring. Orion, whose own head was now spinning
and getting unusually heavy from the drink, just sat there for a
moment, relieved but in a strange, dreamlike state as the servant
girl walked into the room.

"Come," she said, after looking to make sure that Antiope was
deeply asleep. "We don't have much time."

Orion stared at her, blinking his eyes as he tried, through the
fog of his impaired faculties, to understand what she was telling
him.

"I am the one you are looking for," she said. "I am Carina."
After the Amazons had captured the gentle Athenian girl, once she
was old enough, they tried in every way they knew to turn her into
one of them. As with all their captive recruits, they began by
teaching her the art of combat, hand-to-hand and with every type of
weapon, even the heavy axe. But her trainers, including Antiope
herself, could not once incite Carina to strike out at an opponent,
no matter how many times they punished her, often very painfully.
Finally, three years into the fruitless and frustrating endeavor, they
gave up. She would never become one of them, and they hated her

for it. So they made her a slave to serve them, heaping insults and slaps on her while she did. Every day Carina planned ways to escape, but no opportunity ever had presented itself until now, when she had overheard the drunken and giddy warriors carelessly speaking about the purpose for which the Eleans had come to the island. Like their queen, they were unworried that the weak-spirited girl could do anything if she knew. But, without thinking twice, Carina crushed juice from the Sleeping Plant into the red wine that she served to Amazon and guest alike. The brown, thorny vine (with purple leaves that closed and went to sleep when touched) was abundant on the island. From the moment she discovered its properties, ten years ago, Carina always had thought of using it to drug her captors to escape when the chance came.

"Carina!" blurted Orion, shaking his head, surprised. He had expected her to be one of the warriors.

"I put nectar from the Sleeping Plant in the wine," she explained, helping Orion to his feet. "It will wear off soon. It is very strong, but its influence is short-lived. We must move quickly. If they catch us, they will kill us."

"I came here with two friends," said Orion. "We have to find them."

"Don't worry," she replied. "I know where they are. Come with me." Then Carina led Orion, his head spinning and legs wobbling, out of the queen's room, down the dark and narrow stone corridor, to the doorway outside the Warrior Dining Hall. Orion looked in. Sleeping Amazons were piled everywhere. Cadmus lay on the couch next to the pool in the same condition under Penthesilea and

Hippolyta, who were flopped over on top of him. Hipponax, the only one still awake, was sitting confused on the couch in the far corner, holding his head and looking at the warriors splayed on the ground around him. His weight had saved him from the full impact of the wine's added ingredient.

Orion crossed the room to Hipponax, walking carefully to avoid stepping on the warriors littered across the pink marble floor. He helped the big man up, and then together they tiptoed through the thick field of bare limbs and torsos to gather Cadmus from among the pile of beautiful bodies. Unable to revive him, Hipponax slung Cadmus over his shoulder and followed Orion (who had gathered an axe from the ground) out of the hall.

Then Carina led them out of the palace and into the jungle. Still suffering the effects of the Sleeping Plant and slipping on the muddy ground below, they stumbled along as fast as they could through the dense vegetation, heading towards their ship. Orion and his friends had not gotten much further than halfway, when Antiope, having woken and raised the alarm, stormed out of the palace and into the jungle, leading the fifty or so warriors she was able to revive. Furiously intent on preventing any escape, the Amazons, shrieking as they went, ran with wild abandon along the familiar route, often slipping and falling and running into trees because they were still groggy.

The Eleans, led by Carina, having increased their own pace as the war cries neared, burst out of the vegetation onto the beach, three hundred yards to the left of where the five Amazon craft sat with their prows pulled onto the shore and their sterns in the water. As the Eleans raced along the sand towards the boats, they could hear the wild shrieks closing fast, directly there, from inside the dense green.

Panting, the fleeing four reached the Amazon vessels. Hipponax placed Cadmus, still dead to the world, inside the closest, and then he and Carina began pushing its front half off the beach into the water. Meanwhile, Orion, swinging hard with the stolen axe, hacked holes in the bottoms of the four other boats.

Fully expecting that arrows would fly out towards him at any moment, Orion slung the axe away into the sea and waded through the cold, waist-high water to join the others, already in the launched craft. Helped by the big man, he pulled himself up over the side, and then the two sat down across from each other (Orion to port and Hipponax to starboard) and began rowing. Meanwhile, Carina tried to revive Cadmus, who was resting below the prow.

The Amazons (who actually had been much further away than Orion had guessed from their piercing cries) burst out of the jungle onto the beach just as the Eleans pulled the Amazon boat alongside their own ship, waiting where they had left it, fifty yards from the shore.

The tribeswomen ran for their remaining craft, still parked on the sand. Discovering that they had been scuttled, the warriors held out their bows, placed arrows, drew the strings back, and launched volley after volley of bronze-tipped death. But not one shaft came close, their usually sure aim impaired by the effects of the Sleeping Plant mixed with wine and by their shrieking fury. The rain of arrows flew harmlessly wide and over, all the while that the intended victims loaded into their ship, quickly drew up the anchor, and unfurled the sail. Slowly, as the wind caught in the white sheet painted with the blue dolphin (now made silver by starlight), the Eleans' ship began pulling away.

Now the Amazons were reduced to hisses, growls, and howls, as they stood powerless on the sand watching the Athenian merchant vessel escape from their island carrying the despised servant girl and the objects of their awakened desire. As soon as the ship disappeared, the savage women ran into the jungle again, this time to retrieve the rest of their sisterhood. Together, they would board the remaining vessels, moored on the other side of the island, and give chase. Smaller and more nimble than any Athenian ship, especially one lugging cargo, these boats would surely allow the Amazons to catch their prey before they reached Athens. Then, there on the seas, the warriors would make them pay.

Fortunately, the Amazons never found the Eleans, who sailed for Athens directly across the gaping middle of the traveled oceans rather than around the edges of their basins as most everyone did at this time of year to avoid being caught in the open by a storm.

But again Poseidon was kind to the Eleans, providing them with smooth waters and favorable winds. And before they knew it, they were standing with Carina and her tearful parents at the center of the Athenian Council Chamber's green-marble debate floor, surrounded by almost the entire Athenian Council. Save for Nicias and Alcibiades, its members (discarding all their previous ceremony and pretense towards the Eleans) had left their benches in the gallery and were milling excitedly around the heroes.

"Athens is indeed grateful for your service," declared Cleon, voicing what most felt. "You have returned its daughter to Athens and, by doing so, proven your worth. We need no further evidence that Zeus favors you and that you carry his word. If you convince Sparta to observe the truce, Athens will participate in the Olympic Games."

Chapter Seven

COMING INTO PLACE

The Eleans had lodged in the home of Pytheas and his daughters the two nights before leaving to rescue Carina. Orion and Aria, though utterly compelled by the other's physical beauty, had realized that their manners and spirits were even more perfectly matched than their bodies, and Medea's relentless pursuit of Cadmus had provided Pytheas and Hipponax with more than a few laughs.

Now, Pytheas once more welcomed the Eleans to stay in his home, this time more as family than as honored guests. In the evening, Aria and Medea prepared a fine meal, and everyone sat down to enjoy it in the andron; the rectangular room near the front of the house was furnished with couches along its blue walls, low tables laden with refreshment in front of the couches, and a life-sized white-marble statue of the goddess Athena standing in the corner. Meant for entertaining guests, in most households the andron was off limits to the females of the family. But Pytheas did not treat his daughters like most Athenian women. Their mother had died giving birth to Medea, and he had lovingly raised them, on his own, to be strong and independent equals with men. He had even employed a private tutor to educate them from the age of seven, when Athenian boys began their study. And, contrary to custom, the girls always had been allowed to attend dinners in the andron, where they were encouraged to render and debate their opinions on all subjects with their father and his guests.

As dinner continued, it became clear that none of the magic between Orion and Aria had disappeared and that Cadmus was only adding fuel to Medea's fire, the more he resisted her advances while boasting about the alluring Amazons fighting over him.

The night wore on, and Callinus arrived to perform as some small measure of thanks to the Eleans. His music, able to touch the hardest heart, had not been heard in the fifteen years since Carina was taken. But now, first with the wild, eerie sound of his panpipes and then with the strings of his lyre, he filled the andron and the rest of Pytheas' house with haunting melodies. The unspeakable depth and passion of his music was born out of longing for his daughter, her return to him, and the bottling of his creative instincts for all the years they had remained clouded by grief. And by the end, not one eye was dry, performer and audience, even as Demosthenes entered on the strum of the last note.

The great general had come to tell the Eleans what to expect when they arrived at the grim reality that was Sparta, the land of extremes located near the bottom of the Peloponnesian Peninsula. Its winters were cold and summers hot. But if the weather was harsh, the people were more so, all regard for individuality replaced by sternly enforced indoctrination, directed at producing absolute conformity and unquestioning service to the military state and often reflected by a universal hatred of foreigners.

Spartan society was divided into three main classes. The Spartiates, those able to trace their bloodline back to the city's original inhabitants, were at the top, citizens with full rights. Below them were the Perioeci, descendants of the first dwellers of the fertile plains immediately around Sparta. Free men without the full rights of citizenship, the Perioeci were treated as inferior by the Spartiates, yet they could join the army or conduct trades. At the bottom of the ladder were the despised Helots—the enslaved people from beyond the city's immediate ring—who lived on and farmed the Laconian and Messenian plains for the benefit of those above them. Though the Helots outnumbered the free Spartans ten to one, they had no rights and were treated viciously by their masters, who felt the constant threat that the slaves would revolt.

Spartiate males made up most of the army. In fact, they were forbidden from holding any other occupation. Life for them, from the first, was spent in constant pursuit of military excellence. At birth, babies were examined by state officials and if found weak, killed. At age seven, Spartiate boys, along with those Perioeci chosen for service, were taken from their mothers and placed in military schools called Agoge. Life there was harsh. The boys lived in packs under the supervision of the older candidates between their age and twenty. The appalling living conditions (little food and poor shelter) and the constant hazing were designed solely to prepare candidates for the fearsome Spartan infantry by teaching them to endure pain and suffering, indoctrinating them to fear disgrace more than death, and by fashioning their bodies into robust instruments of destruction. At twenty, worthy Agoge graduates were invited to join a military barracks, where they lived with their fellow soldiers—and not with their wives—until they turned thirty, though life as a Spartan warrior continued until retirement at sixty.

Spartiate women also lived very different lives from the far more sheltered and restricted existences of women in other parts of Greece. They, like male Spartiates, were examined as babies and if found wanting, killed. As young girls, they were encouraged to exercise (gymnastics, jumping, running, and even wrestling), which accounted for their legendary beauty, in addition to making them strong and healthy enough to survive childbirth and produce suitable male babies for the state to fashion into warriors. Grown Spartiate women also enjoyed considerable freedom and autonomy. Spartiate men were mostly busy fulfilling their military obligations at home or abroad, and Spartiate women, unlike women in other cities, had to conduct all household business and manage estates in their husbands' absence, while their men were alive, or completely without them if they had been killed in battle.

Traditionally, for about two and a half centuries, Spartan government had been a strange combination of monarchy and oligarchy, open only to Spartiate males. At the top, two coequal kings inherited their positions, one each from among the members of the two royal houses. Together, they led the army and presided over the Assembly of twenty-eight senior citizens, appointed for life from Spartiate aristocrats. The Assembly, under direction of the two kings, was responsible for voting yes or no on matters as important as declaring war. The Assembly also elected the Ephorate. The five men of this body served for only one year but exerted immense influence because they had the power to veto any of the Assembly's decisions, and they could even depose the kings with sufficient divine proof from omens or oracles.

But just over twelve years ago, Sparta's kings, Archidamus and Lycurgus, abolished the Assembly and the Ephorate by turning the tables on them. Lycurgus, then sixty, convinced his much younger counterpart that he had been visited in his dreams by Ares, the war god, and told to do so. Brutish Archidamus, already at twenty-one the most admired and feared soldier, easily convinced the rest of the troops to back them. A year later, Lycurgus claimed that Ares had visited again, this time instructing him to invade Athens to prevent the Athenians from destroying Sparta. But Lycurgus, too old for war and too cunning to leave matters unattended at home, remained in the city in command of several thousand men, while Archidamus, always eager for a fight, led the rest of the Spartan army out of the homeland to start the present war.

The last foray of this conflict ended months ago—when General Demosthenes led the defense of the Dipylon Gateway. Then, as Archidamus withdrew his men from Athens, already he was planning his return. But he was even more determined now that

Lycurgus had, upon his coming home, seized the opportunity to
work on his mind. Constantly, the older monarch bent the younger
to a simple, though brutishly effective, instrument of his will. And
at the exact moment that Demosthenes sat in Pytheas' andron
warning the Eleans how difficult it would be to get Sparta to agree
to the Olympic Games, Lycurgus was fashioning Archidamus to his
latest needs.

The andron of Lycurgus' palace measured fifty feet by thirty. A
white-marble statue of Ares adorned each of its four corners, and
the walls were painted deep Spartan Red. The color on the walls
matched the cushions on the four couches around the low wooden
table at the center of the room. There the kings sat talking, directly
across from one another.

Lycurgus had an average build for a Spartan of his years.
Though balding at the front, he still wore his gray hair plaited long
at the back. His bearded face was wide, hard, and cunning. His eye-
slits were long and narrow, with sagging bags under each dark,
callous instrument of vision. He certainly never reflected the same
physical presence as Archidamus, whose massive frame and baboon-like features were intimidating even to his fellow Spartans.
Yet, between the two, Lycurgus clearly dominated. "One of our
spies has just returned from Athens. He informs me that soon a
young traveler will come to us claiming that Zeus has sent him. He
will ask us to declare a truce to participate in the Olympic Games
in the hope that they will bring lasting peace throughout Greece."

"Of course we will refuse," replied Archidamus, expecting that
his answer would please his mentor, who instead shot him a dis-

dainful glance. Though Archidamus, fearless and with utter disregard for human suffering, was a useful puppet, Lycurgus had always despised the younger king for his lack of wile. Now, once again, Archidamus had proven his stupidity by speaking too soon rather than waiting for Lycurgus to reveal his true purpose.

"On the contrary, Archidamus," Lycurgus lectured. "We certainly will agree to participate."

"What!" exclaimed Archidamus, shocked that Lycurgus was insisting on a course so seemingly at odds with the one they had pursued for over a decade.

"We will never take Athens while Demosthenes leads its defense," explained Lycurgus. "But do not forget that he is still their athletic champion. He will go to Olympia, assured by the truce, leaving that blundering coward Nicias to defend Athens. But then, while you compete at the games as Sparta's champion and destroy Demosthenes in front of all Greece, our army will launch a surprise attack to take the city. And even if our raid is not at first successful, when you dispose of the hero of the Island of Wasps, it will break Athens' spirit and cause their allies to see which side they really should back. After that, it will just be a matter of time before *the great democracy* falls."

"But dare we violate the hallowed peace, ordained by Zeus himself?" questioned Archidamus, concerned.

"About that, we need not worry," Lycurgus answered. "Ares has assured me he will intervene to protect us from Zeus. It seems a new order is coming to both Heaven and Earth."

❧

A week later, the three Eleans rode over Mount Parnon, east-ernmost of the three lofty mountain ranges that bordered Sparta, just miles to its north, forming a massive three-sided protective barrier that allowed the Spartans to look up and see enemies com-ing. The city lay below, at the upper tip of the Eurotas Valley, which spread out south behind it in a flat, fertile triangle. The River Eurotas, to the west of the city, ran southward through the widening plain, down towards the sea, twenty-five miles away.

The Eleans came down from Parnon and started across the rough, flat terrain, the last remaining stretch standing between them and their destination. And as the friends drew to within eight hundred yards of the city, they were bewildered by what they saw. Demosthenes had warned them what Sparta would be like, but still the reality seemed worse than they had imagined, and it was hard to believe that a place such as this could rival grand Athens. Sparta had no perimeter walls. Instead, a ring of rectangular wooden army barracks enclosed a sprawling village in which winding dirt roads and wooden structures surrounded a puny Acropolis. Atop the Acropolis sat two modest stone palaces and the temple, with bronze-plated walls, previously dedicated to Athena but now given over to Ares. Even from this distance, it was undeniable that Sparta was essentially an armed camp, filled with drilling and patrolling soldiers and with sullen Helots serving their masters.

As the Eleans rode closer, to within a hundred yards, the sense of bewilderment grew into anxiety, gripping deep inside. Suddenly, it was shaken right out, replaced by fear in the pit of their stomachs. A column of twenty Spartan soldiers, two across and ten long, with Archidamus and General Brasidas at the front, marched out from behind one of the rectangular barracks, in full battle dress over the white tunics worn under the Spartan Red robes flowing down their backs.

The Spartans turned and headed right for the Eleans, who now slowed their horses to a walk—the three friends each swallowing hard as they continued forward to meet the sentries striding aggressively towards them. The soldiers looked dreadfully similar to those the Eleans had fought in the mountains, weeks ago, when they had first traveled to Athens.

The two groups advanced to within ten yards of each other, then stopped as Archidamus held up his hand. The column of soldiers reformed into one flat line across, nine on each side of their two leaders. Now they raised and cocked their spears above their heads, ready to let fly at the riders.

The Eleans, so that they would not be made out as thieves, were riding different horses from those taken from Brasidas and his men. But the three friends, especially with Hipponax in the mix, formed too distinct a picture. Brasidas recognized them. Then the Spartan general leaned over to Archidamus and whispered. Archidamus' eyes excited cruel as he listened.

When Brasidas was done, Archidamus whispered back to him and then looked up at the mounted Eleans. "What business do you have here?" demanded the king. He would find out if these were in fact the same men as Brasidas suspected. And if they were, they would receive a fitting death.

From the look of the Spartans, a bad end seemed imminent. Orion realized that if he did not speak clearly and directly now, he would never get the chance to deliver his message. "We have been sent to ask Sparta to participate in the Olympic Games."

"Do not cast!" Archidamus shouted to his men.

Minutes later, the three Eleans, now treated as honored guests, sat with the two Spartan kings on the four couches at the center of Lycurgus' andron; the low table in front of them was set with a feast. Cadmus, Hipponax, and Archidamus, each occupying his own couch, in a prodigious show of excess, increasingly challenged one another to a contest of gluttony.

Meanwhile, Lycurgus turned to Orion, finalizing the matter at hand. "This war has grown old. For a long time I've wanted to make peace, but I could never find the right way. You realize that the troubles only started so that we could protect our own homeland from being invaded."

"It's such a shame that Zeus did not command this sooner," replied Orion, believing that fawning Lycurgus was sincere. "Imagine how much trouble could have been saved."

"Yes, imagine," replied Lycurgus, gushing with his true purpose in mind.

The Spartans had been convinced far more easily than Orion expected, and so he asked again to make sure that Lycurgus was in fact adopting the most essential element of the pact. "You really will observe a truce from now until the end of the Olympic Games next summer?"

"Of course," replied Lycurgus, putting his hand on Orion's shoulder to reassure the young shepherd as he finished setting the trap. "And not only will Sparta compete, but as a gesture of our goodwill, instead of the Hellanodikes, we will host the games at Olympia. Let everyone come enjoy Spartan hospitality."

"That won't be necessary," replied Orion. "Besides, the Hellanodikes will not relinquish their role. They have…"

Lycurgus, his hand still resting on Orion's shoulder as he poured on the charm, did not allow Orion to finish. "I insist. We have much to reconcile with our friends in the rest of Greece. We will host everyone at Olympia once the games begin, or we will not participate. We must do this right or not at all."

❧

The Eleans returned to Athens to relay the Spartan condition. Athens agreed, believing it better to have the games with the Spartans administering them than not at all.

The next day, the three friends started the journey to Elis to take the news to the Hellanodikes, this time riding around the mountains in which they had lost Aeneas and then down towards their home.

Comforted to at last be in familiar surroundings, they arrived at the farm late one evening. Cadmus' parents gave them an excited welcome, but soon the mood turned sad when Aeneas' fate came to light. Then Cadmus' parents made dinner for the remaining three travelers and listened to everything else they had to tell.

After dark, the meal done, Hipponax and Orion left the farm and rode for Elis proper, parting company at the edge of town, each continuing on to his separate destination. The big man went to surprise his wife. Orion headed directly to visit Aeneas' mother.

Orion knocked on her door. With one look at his face, she needed no words to know what news he brought. Instantly, she dropped to the ground, tears flooding down. But still she did not make a sound, even as Orion (crying too) lifted her up to a chair and tried to offer what comfort he could.

Rocking back and forth in the chair, she sobbed the rest of the night, on into the middle of the morning, when Orion fetched the neighbors to care for her so that he could leave to visit the Hellano-dikes. He apologized again, promised to return to talk with her when he was done, and then left. But he never saw her again. As Orion walked away from her house, Aeneas' mother gulped down an infusion of hemlock. Sensing that her son would not return, she had (days after the wolves took Aeneas in the wooded gorge) gone into the countryside to gather the fatal herb in preparation for this moment.

An hour later, lying in the same bed in which she had given birth to Aeneas, she gasped for the last time and went to meet him. Meanwhile, Orion stood before the ten men in purple robes, at the center of the floor in their round hall.

Now that Orion had done all of the work, the Hellanodikes

were only too happy to sanction the games (to claim credit for themselves) and push him out of the way, even forbidding him from competing. And they did not listen when he warned them that the Spartans would assume the role of hosts after arriving at Olympia. Instead, the Hellanodikes believed they could persuade the Spartans (and everyone else) otherwise. The sacred duty, after all, always had fallen to their order.

Immediately, the Hellanodikes (wrapped in the fervor of their own importance rather than the purpose of the games) dispatched heralds wearing wreaths of olive leaves on their crowns and carrying wooden staffs adorned with the official dove emblem. And the heralds traveled throughout the Greek mainland, announcing the Olympic Truce and summoning the people and the champions from each locale. The people who heard the news spread the message wider. Soon word of the games burned across the entire country like wildfire, and it even spread across the seas to the islands of the Aegean and the Mediterranean and the Greek colonies around their shores.

❧

While the entire land vibrated with news of the impending games, the ten Hellanodikes commanded the people of Elis to prepare the nearby site at Olympia, located on a grassy plain between the Alpheus and Cladeus Rivers (near their confluence) and surrounded by rolling, wooded hills. It had no permanent inhabitants and was not used except for the Olympic Games. Even with

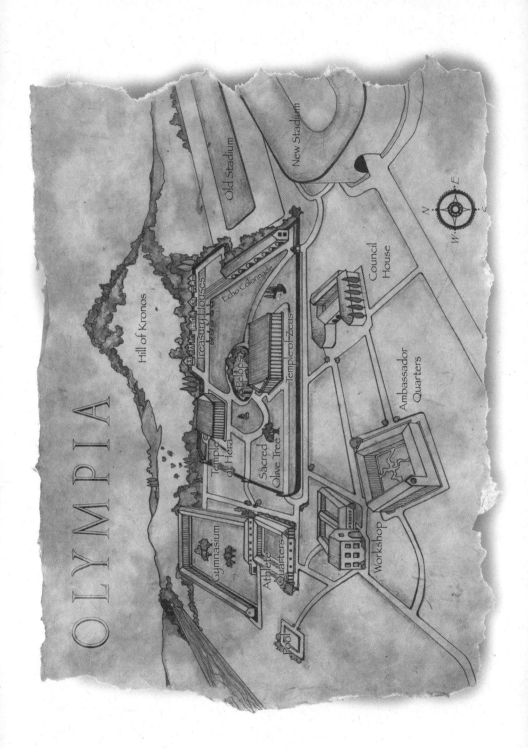

the usual lapse of four years between competitions, the grounds, stadium, and other buildings required substantial attention to make them suitable. But now that twelve years had passed since the last time the grandest of all athletic contests was held, the impressive complex needed considerably more cleaning, clearing, patching, and resurfacing so that it would look its best.

At the heart of Olympia was the walled precinct known as the Sacred Grove, around which the layout of the entire magnificent site was based. And at the center of the Sacred Grove (facing east) stood the bright-white, Doric-style Temple of Zeus, in whose honor the Games always had been held. It had thirty-four massive columns. The triangular roof pediments (both at the front of the structure and at the back) were filled with marble sculptures depicting the deeds of past mortal heroes. On the grass all around the temple stood dozens of statues of past champions and one, perhaps the most finely crafted of all these, dedicated to Nike, winged patroness of victory.

Fifteen more buildings shared the Sacred Grove with the Temple of Zeus. A smaller temple dedicated to Hera, wife of Zeus, had forty columns, each different from every other. The monument built to honor the hero Pelops, mortal founder of the games, sat between the two temples. The Echo Colonnade, roofed by terracotta tiles, gained its name from the fact that its unusual acoustics could repeat an echo seven times. Twelve Treasury Houses, resembling little temples, were used to store precious offerings from the various cities to Zeus.

The wooded Hill of Kronos loomed to the north of the Sacred

Grove, behind its retaining wall. It was here, at the dawn of time, that Zeus was reputed to have become leader of the gods, and therefore it was a logical choice next to which to build the complex to hold games in his honor.

The Old Stadium lay to the east of the Sacred Grove. Its dirt competition floor had been the scene of many exciting events, witnessed from its surrounding grass banks by thousands of spectators. Now it had given way to the New Stadium, a massive bowl erected in stone, south from it, over the ground of the Hippodrome. Originally, the Old Stadium hosted all but the horse and chariot races, which thundered around the Hippodrome's dirt track, surrounded by its own crowded grass banks. But roughly twenty years ago, the functions of the two facilities had been combined into the more impressive New Stadium, where all events now took place.

The Council House, seat of the Olympic Senate, stood directly to the south of the Sacred Grove. In its two high halls, each rounded at the front, the ambassadors sent by the participating cities met to discuss the format and rules, subject to the final decision of the ten men in purple robes, whose colonnade-lined quarters were attached across the back of the two Senate Chambers. Wedged between the two great halls and the Hellanodike Quarters was an open-air courtyard that contained a gigantic bronze statue of Zeus holding two menacing thunderbolts in his hands. Before it, the athletes and Hellanodikes, who also acted as the judges for all competitions, took their solemn oaths to honor fair play.

The luxurious Ambassador Quarters sat west of the Council House, off the southwest corner of the Sacred Grove. Under its terra-cotta tile roof, the two-story-tall structure easily could accommodate over a hundred guests in its rooms, which wrapped around a courtyard garden containing a clover-shaped pond.

The Workshop stood to the north of the Ambassador Quarters. The fine craftsmen who worked on the complex stayed here for the duration of their projects, and it was in its courtyards that the sculptor Phidias created the spectacular statue of Zeus that now resided in the interior of the massive temple at the center of the Sacred Grove.

The Athlete Quarters and the Gymnasium stood to the north of the Workshop. Both courtyards were used for training. The square Athlete Quarters' courtyard was used for combat sports, and the rectangular Gymnasium's was used for running and throwing events. On both buildings, spectators could watch from beneath the same surrounding covered Ionic colonnades under which the competitors trained in bad weather. The main functional difference between the two buildings, which also accounted for the smaller structure's name, was that the Athlete Quarters contained accommodations for the competitors and their trainers. The covered colonnades surrounding its courtyard had rooms at their back. And a door led from the Athlete Quarters' northwest corner to the two-story dormitory wedged between it and the south perimeter wall of the Gymnasium.

Outside the training area, there was a square pool for the athletes to soak their bodies in the hope of restoring them after

rigorous competition. It was reputed to absorb rejuvenating properties through its plaster from the soil below. And it was said that if
you stuck only one of your hands into the pool, that the immersed
hand, over the course of years, would show notably fewer signs of
aging than the hand that had not been immersed.

Behind the pool, at its western edge, Olympia was bounded by
the River Cladeus. It ran northeast and then wrapped around the
Gymnasium to continue sharper east behind the north face of the
Hill of Kronos, separating the compound from the plains and
wooded hills on the other side. The Alpheus, lined by olives and
pines, sat a few hundred yards to the south of the entire complex,
across its bottom edge. Beyond this river, too, the grassy flat
continued and then folded into more rolling, wooded hills.

Chapter Eight

LET THE GAMES BEGIN

Hundreds of cities usually attended the Olympic Games. But on this occasion the scent of war was too pungent for most, and in the end only people from eight locales—one island and seven cities (Sparta, Athens, Argos, Mantinea, Thebes, Corinth, and Elis)—decided that they would come to Olympia.

Exactly one month from the first full moon in August, when the games were scheduled to open, the impressive complex was ready. And the Hellanodikes, who spoke for Elis in addition to running the games, received the ambassadors and athletic champions sent by Athens, Argos, Mantinea, Thebes, and Corinth. Some had come by land, but most had chosen not to cross the rugged terrain. Instead, they had traveled up the Alpheus River in ships (now docked on her banks) from the waters of the Ionian Sea, roughly ten miles away.

Three hundred unarmed Amazons rode in the next day on horses they had caught and tamed on the plains to the east of the Black Sea. Women never had been invited to compete. But, having heard of the games from a recent captive, the female warriors ventured to Olympia insisting that their champion, Penthesilea, be allowed to participate. And the ambassadors agreed with the Hellanodikes to let her into the competition to boost the number of athletes since so few places had sent champions.

The two Spartan kings marched in the next day. Coming from the east, they suddenly emerged from behind the New Stadium, leading a column of nine hundred soldiers, all wearing crested helmets and bronze armor and carrying massive blood-red and shining bronze shields, long spears, and short swords for hacking.

Immediately, everyone else (besides the Amazons) protested, and the Hellanodikes ordered the Spartans to surrender their weapons. Bearing arms always had been considered a flagrant violation of the sacred truce and was forbidden. Backed by their nine hundred fearsome warriors, Lycurgus and Archidamus—rather than obey the Hellanodikes' mandate to relinquish the offending articles —insisted that the older king assume all duties and authority from the men in purple robes. The Spartans, who had conditioned their participation upon acting as hosts, clearly meant to enforce this proviso under threat of severe force. But force was not necessary. Athens spoke up to acknowledge the condition, and the other participants agreed to honor it. Even the Hellanodikes (who never before had relinquished their role to anyone) accepted, lest the games not take place, supplanted by violence. In exchange, Lycurgus would allow them, under his supervision and control, to act in a diminished capacity as event judges.

With the matter decided and the games to go on, the Hellano-dikes assigned each competitor to one of the small rooms under the north colonnade of the Athlete Quarters; the front doors of the athletes' rooms faced the courtyard and their trainers' rooms on the other side of the building, under the south colonnade.

However, only six athletes actually occupied their designated housing. Archidamus stayed in the Ambassador Quarters. And Penthesilea rode with her sisters into the hills to the north of Olympia; there they could remain separate from everyone else and sleep under the summer stars as their tribe had done when it roamed the wild lands.

Now all eight athletes set hard to preparing themselves for the upcoming competition. The seven from the cities trained relentlessly in the open-air courtyards of the Gymnasium and Athlete Quarters, watched from under the respective colonnades by everyone else, including the stone-faced Spartan soldiers, who even then did not relinquish their armaments. Penthesilea prepared in the hills by wrestling against others from her tribe, including her closest rival, blonde-haired Hippolyta.

Ten days before the opening ceremony, a trickle of spectators began flowing into Olympia from each of the six participating cities besides Sparta, which sent none. Three days later, the trickle turned into a steady stream. In four days more, it swelled to a flood, and now the Alpheus was packed with boats, and Olympia pulsed with the energy of twenty thousand people, almost exclusively men. Married women were forbidden at the games, and only a handful of the most daring maidens generally attended.

The spectators from the six cities (Athens, Argos, Mantinea, Thebes, Corinth, and Elis) erected their tents on the grassy plain below the bottom edge of the Olympia compound, north and south of the Alpheus and on the rolling hills further south of her. But wartime, though temporarily halted by the Olympic Truce, had made everyone suspicious of people different from themselves. So the spectators from the six cities pitched their canvases next to others originating from the same place, forming six distinct districts of uniform nationality. And no one ventured outside of his separate precinct to that set up by the people from another locale. Nor did anyone venture to the Old Stadium—where performers, artists, merchants, and food-sellers from the six competing nationalities (besides Spartan and Amazon) had been allowed to erect their stalls over the ground which in years past was used for competition. Instead, each group of spectators, keeping to its area, feasted amongst itself, while everyone waited for the opening ceremony.

On the morning that the games began, a crowd of spectators, divided by nationality, stood shoulder-to-shoulder, deep back on both sides of the path that ran from the Council House to the New Stadium; the spectators marveled at the procession traveling between them along the path. At the front, walking four abreast, were twelve maidens, all sixteen years old, blonde hair loose down their backs. They were dressed in long, flowing white gowns and carried baskets filled with yellow rose petals, which they cast on the ground below their feet.

Behind the maidens, two abreast, walked the ten Hellanodikes; regardless of having been humbled by the Spartans, the men in purple royal robes were acting as if the whole event was more about them than anything else.

Last, following behind the white gowns and the purple robes, in single file, dressed in pristine white tunics, walked the athletic champions who had come to challenge the Spartan king. The colorful seven, each magnificent in his own way, were all solemn, having just sworn the Olympic Oath before the giant bronze statue of Zeus in the courtyard of the Council House. They just looked straight ahead and did not engage the crowd, even though the spectators increasingly shouted encouragement to their favorites with every step that the procession traveled further down the path between the foaming sea of fans.

The procession reached outside the arch of the vaulted entrance, set flush in the rounded western end of the arena. The exterior wall of the massive stone oval loomed sixty feet above. One of the athletes in the procession already had competed and won at the Olympic Games. But for the other six, this was the first time gracing the grand event. Yet each of the seven athletes in the procession now dreamed equally of snatching glory. And the full measure of desire soared in all of their hearts that they were about to begin the journey to become Olympic Grand Champion, to be revered and honored throughout the entire Greek world and perhaps, if they were valiant enough, to live on in stories passed down through time.

The procession walked into the dark, ten-foot-wide, vaulted

entrance tunnel. The fifteen-foot-high walls of both sides joined above them in a rounded arch that ran below the vibrating terraces for the full twenty-five yards of the tunnel's length.

Soon the front of the procession reached the far mouth, flooded with light where the tunnel connected seamlessly to the inside of the bowl. There the maidens and everyone else behind them halted for a moment. The awesome sight of the interior of the packed and throbbing arena stood before them.

The oval, grass-covered competition floor ran a hundred yards in the distance to the other rounded end and spread fifty yards across the middle. On both sides, on the edge of its wide midpoint, sat a row of ten ornate white-marble chairs complete with tall backs, armrests, and legs carved in the shape of the paws of a lion. The two Spartan kings occupied the two seats in the middle of the otherwise unfilled row to the right. Ten ambassadors (two each from Athens, Corinth, Argos, Mantinea, and Thebes) sat in the row of ten ornate seats to the left. Two trumpeters stood on both sides of the ambassadors' chairs. Outside of them, shield-to-shield, the nine hundred fully armed and armored Spartan soldiers, bronze glinting in the morning sun, ringed the rest of the competition floor, save over the entrance and row of chairs across the way.

Immediately behind the rows of seats and the ring of soldiers was a waist-high wall, gapped in places to allow the twenty thousand spectators access from the arena floor into the twenty layered terraces of stone seating. Like a series of angled steps, these ran to the top, all around the giant oval, even wrapping over the entrance tunnel, the single means of entering or leaving the stadium, above which now sat the Amazon clan, secluded in their own section. The rest of the terraces were filled to capacity with the crowd of almost exclusively male spectators from every attending city except Sparta, sitting distinctly divided by nationality, gasping with excitement, expecting the first glimpse of the athletes.

The procession stepped forward, out of the tunnel, and started onto the stadium grass. The trumpeters raised their horns and sounded a long blast. The spectators, as one, surged to their feet from their terrace seats, for the first time acting together, driven by the same universal passion. The pure and instinctive thrill that in the next days they would witness the epic battles of the most noble of all competitions. Soon great hopes and dreams would rise and fall on the grand central stage of the arena floor, right before their eyes.

The twelve maidens, still casting yellow rose petals from their baskets, led the ten Hellanodikes and seven athletes to the middle of the grass; and the entire procession turned to face the Spartan kings, still reposed in the ornate white-marble chairs on the right edge of the competition area.

Lycurgus rose from his seat, lifting his hands to calm the buzzing crowd. All fell dead quiet as the spectators sat back down. Then he cast his strong voice into the silence. "It is with great pleasure that I welcome you all to the greatest Olympics ever held."

Lycurgus turned to acknowledge Cleon, elderly Speaker of the Athenian Council, sitting with the rest of the ambassadors on the other side of the arena floor. "Before we begin the festivities, I would like to take a moment to pay special thanks to the dignitaries from Athens for participating in these games. Let us hope they bring us closer."

Cleon, wishful that Lycurgus' gesture was indeed the beginning of healing the rift between their two societies, rose from his seat and bowed graciously to acknowledge the seemingly sincere overture. Despite Cleon's advocacy of an aggressive war strategy, he and all Athenians craved an end to hostilities.

Lycurgus, sensing his optimism, nodded reassuringly back as the Athenian sat down. For the time being, it would suit the Spartan king's purpose for his counterpart to wallow in the illusion of possible reconciliation.

Then Lycurgus' voice rose strong again to the whole stadium. "Now, without further ceremony, I declare the games officially open."

The trumpeters sounded another blast. The maidens turned and paraded out of the stadium the way they had come in. The ten Hellanodikes joined the Spartan kings, four seated on either side of the monarchs, one standing at each end of their row of chairs. Meanwhile, Ibycus (the painfully slim Elean announcer with long hair and a flair for high drama), wearing his blue tunic, pushed past the ring of Spartans, among whom he had been uncomfortably waiting. Then the flamboyant showman strode to the center of the grass to stand next to the seven athletes there.

"These magnificent competitors come to you from near," Ibycus began, addressing the entire crowd. "They come to you from far. They come to you from all of Greece and even from beyond. Now, are you ready to meet them?"

"Yes," the powerful reply instantly vibrated from the spectators in the terraces, again acting as one.

Ibycus, more than a little pleased at how easily he had put the audience under his spell, was in his element; and his gestures, gyrations, and voice fluctuations became even more exaggerated. "Then, without further delay, here they are. First out of the gate, built for speed not power, I give you Argive of Argos."

The twenty-eight-year-old teacher, who lived the ideal of a healthy body and healthy mind, five-foot-ten, 170 pounds, stepped forward from among the group of athletes and raised his right hand to wave to the cheering spectators from his home. His face was fairly pleasing. He had a somewhat small but wide nose; dark, determined eyes; a strong eyebrow ridge; and straight, black hair that he wore cropped close to his dome-shaped head. Argive was not really his name. Rather, it was what people from Argos were called. But he had insisted that he be titled in the official records as such, since he came more to honor his people than himself. Their city long ago had been one of the foremost in all Greece but had declined when the Spartans wrested control of the Peloponnese from them, some 180 years before. Argos, refusing to fight with the Spartans or against them, had stayed out of the present war between Sparta and Athens.

"He is built to destroy and has a heart to match," continued Ibycus. "Representing the city of Mantinea, here is Memnon, the traveling warrior from Ethiopia." Thirty-eight-year-old Memnon, cracking his knuckles, stepped forward to cheers from the spectators from Mantinea. He was a fine five-foot-eleven specimen of his native Africa. His face was hard and strong, as was his clean-shaven head, supported by a thick neck that connected down to the square-set 218 pounds of pure, compact muscle with which he had fought many battles as a mercenary for a variety of employers all across the foreign lands. Now the people of Mantinea, not having produced a suitable champion of their own, had, for a price, named him as theirs. Mantinea, a fledgling democracy, was traditionally one of Sparta's enemies, and it supported Athens in the war outside.

"He can crush rocks with his bare hands," proclaimed Ibycus to the stadium, "Konon of Corinth."

As the spectators from Corinth cheered, the twenty-four-year-old quarry worker, six-foot-five, 240 pounds (a long build of dense muscle derived from years of hard labor), stepped forward and crumbled a stone to sand in his gnarled right paw. His wavy, black hair was cut two inches long for the competition so that no one could hold it, but still a few strands, having escaped the barber, cascaded over the top of his forehead. All the while, he wore a goofy, buck-teethed smile on his simple face, which resembled a larger and far less intelligent version of Argive's. Corinth, a sea-faring city, coveted Athens' position as the foremost trading center in the Greek world, and it willingly sided with Sparta.

"As tall, wide, and strong as a giant oak," Ibycus announced, "please welcome Herak of Thebes."

Herak, twenty-three, six-foot-six, 270 pounds, stepped forward to receive the cheers of the spectators from his home. The boorish bodyguard of one of the richest men in Thebes was the largest competitor, though his massive dimensions were covered by soft, rounded tissue over his deep, bullish muscles. His features and long, straight, ginger-red hair (cinched at the back into a tail) came from his father, who had traveled to the land of Zeus after meeting Greek traders on the high seas near his Nordic home. Thebes, an oligarchy like Sparta, had sided with the blood-red and shining bronze from the start of the present war, and it may well have been at their urging that the Spartan army executed all the prisoners taken at Plataea, their bitter rival. But arrogance and mistreatment, levied on the local population by the Spartan soldiers who stopped in Thebes, had recently worn thin, and the Thebans wondered if they had not made a mistake in backing the fearsome warriors from the south.

"This twenty-five-year-old, olive-skinned savage was not invited, but she came to compete anyway," announced Ibycus. "Here is the wild and unpredictable Penthesilea of the Amazons."

Penthesilea, six feet, 165 pounds of supple muscle, growled at Ibycus as she stepped forward to howls from the Amazon spectators. The feral yet alluring female warrior (with catlike face and deep-yellow eyes) had come to test herself against the finest male specimens. She seemed determined to beat them all.

"With a heart as pure as driven snow, he is the man credited by many with reviving the Olympic Games," Ibycus shouted proudly. "Representing Elis, I give you the one, the only, Orion!" After the Hellanodikes forbade Orion from competing at the Olympic Games, he had set to training Hipponax, whom, despite the big man's protest, the men in purple robes had named to take Orion's place as Champion of Elis. But when the Spartans wrested control of the games, Hipponax offered his position to the true champion of his city, and the Spartans, over the Hellanodikes' protest, accepted the substitution, believing that the giant posed a far greater threat to Archidamus than this much smaller replacement.

Twenty-one-year-old Orion, six-foot-one, 210 pounds, stepped forward to polite applause from the entire terrace crowd except the Amazons (who hissed and snarled) and the Eleans (who shouted encouragement). The band of female warriors, especially scar-faced Antiope, would never forget him for escaping their clutches and rescuing Carina. Yet, despite the Amazons, who to large measure were counteracted by the Eleans, no other athlete had received such universal exaltation from the spectators as a whole.

Now, embarrassed by the reception, humble Orion, not having expected anything approaching such a warm welcome from the large number of strangers, nodded his head in grateful acknowledgement. Then, much to his surprise, he spotted Aria among the blur of faces in the Athenian section of the terrace crowd. She was sitting next to her father, Pytheas, and her sister, Medea. And Aria was staring right at Orion. Now he locked eyes with her, and they both felt a rush of pure excitement that even surpassed the power of the moment when they were first entranced by each other in Athens' Agora. It had been six dragging months since they had last seen each other; they had said goodbye with a hug at the mouth of her city's Dipylon Courtyard when Orion left back to Elis to carry hope of the games to the Hellanodikes.

"Next, we have the finest all-around athlete of his generation,"

Ibycus continued, "Demosthenes!" The great savior of Athens had competed at the Olympics on three previous occasions. At age twenty, he was runner up. At age twenty-four, he became Olympic Grand Champion. And at the last games, when Demosthenes was twenty-eight, he was forced to withdraw after a bad crash in the chariot race.

The ruggedly handsome general (forty years old, six-foot-one, 220 perfectly balanced pounds) stepped forward to loud applause from the terraces, which somewhat muted the ill words screamed at him by all but one of the scowling Amazons. Queen Antiope was quiet. A rage too deep for curses burned for the man who long ago had rendered the disfigurement down the middle of her face and had put her mother in the grave.

Demosthenes, accustomed to receiving adulation, bowed his head confidently to acknowledge those in the stadium crowd who now honored him.

"Last, but most certainly not least," Ibycus announced, "I bring you one of the two great Spartan monarchs, one of your generous hosts, the strong, the determined, the relentless, Archidamus of Sparta."

The six-foot-four, 255-pound, merciless and intimidating, thirty-three-year-old Spartan king (with dark, baboon-like features under long, dark, plaited hair and short beard) rose from his seat and raised his arms triumphantly. He fully expected the same degree of respect as had been granted Demosthenes since it was tradition for the crowd to universally honor the very best athletes regardless of politics in the outside world. Surely everyone knew of his prowess as an overwhelming competitor.

Instead, except from the silent Amazons, he received a universal chorus of boos from the terraces. The hijacking of the competition by the Spartans had offended everyone in the crowd except the she-leopards, ally and enemy alike, as an unforgivable violation of the sacred Olympic Spirit. Besides, many remembered that Archidamus had been disqualified from the competition for aggressiveness outside the rules the last time the games were held, the only previous occasion he ever had participated.

Archidamus was furious. Still the crowd's disapproval rained despite the swelling veins in his neck and reddening face. The impulsive brute was about to lose control and order his troops into the terraces. But Ibycus, rightfully concerned that the king would try to save face in a way that would finish the games before they had begun, shouted to the crowd to divert the spectators' attention. "I see you are all anxious to get to the rules!"

The crowd quieted, not really having heard him above its din but willing to cede the floor to the entertaining master of ceremonies who was frantically waving his arms above his head at the center of the arena floor.

Archidamus, fuming, sat back down.

"There are three preliminary events," Ibycus continued, "a boxing competition to test strength, a chariot race to test speed, and the javelin toss to test accuracy. If any athlete prevails in two of these preliminary events, then he automatically wins the games. But if a different competitor prevails in each preliminary event, we will be treated to a truly amazing spectacle. We will witness, before our very eyes, the three preliminary event winners (boxing, chariot, and javelin) compete against each other in one final event to decide which one of them ascends to the honor of Grand Olympic Champion."

Over the years, the Olympic Games had followed many formats, some similar to the present one and others not quite so, but none designed to favor a particular participant. Yet here, the Spartan kings had chosen the events and structured the competition to practically guarantee Archidamus victory. He was master of all three war-oriented sports, having participated in all of them for years without ever losing, even against much older boys in the Agoge. Now he fully expected to win the first two contests, making short work of his rise to Olympic Grand Champion.

Chapter Nine

THE HOT NIGHT AFTER

S ix weeks before the games, the two Spartan kings had gathered
their army in front of the barracks at home to set the most
destructive elements of their plan in motion. Immediately, five
thousand storm troopers would march south to the sea and board
ships that would land them behind cover of the gentle coastal
mountains on the eastern edge of Attica, directly across from
Athens. There, they would wait hidden among the range's trees until the proper moment came to unleash the storm, while Lycurgus
and Archidamus, with nine hundred of the most vicious warriors,
attended the festival at Olympia. The rest of the army, bolstered to
six thousand by Agoge boys above the age of fourteen, would
remain in Sparta to oversee that all went smoothly should another
city break the truce to attack the homeland. These troops would
also keep the Helots reminded of their place.

Now, as everyone exited the stadium at Olympia after the opening ceremony, the treacherous expedition marched, ten wide and five hundred long, across the Attica plain, heading towards unsuspecting Athens, which lay just seventeen miles in the distance. But this was more than the usual mobilization of the impressive Spartan war machine. Never before had they wheeled along objects similar to the several large wooden devices that their troops, while waiting to attack, had built from their ships' timbers and then, to keep secret, had covered over with white cloth tarpaulins made from the remnant sails.

General Brasidas, leader of the expedition, rode at the front atop his white stallion with gray spots, which had been returned to him by Athens. Mounted Captain Terpander, who months before had stood with spear raised next to the general as they stopped the three Eleans outside Sparta, galloped to join him from his position, fifty rows back in the formation.

"Sir," Terpander reported as he pulled up next to his commander, "the scouts say we will be there tomorrow, exactly as planned."

"Good," responded the general, his jaw tightening with resolve as he glanced at one of the covered objects. "While Archidamus crushes Demosthenes, we will crush his people. For years we struggled to copy such a weapon of terror from the Carthaginians. Isn't it fitting that our engineers discovered how to build it in time for such a promising occasion?"

❧

After the opening ceremony, the different visitors to Olympia settled into their own rhythms. The crowds of spectators (from Athens, Argos, Mantinea, Thebes, Corinth, and Elis) for the most part still kept to their own kind in their separate precincts, feasting amongst others from the same place. However, now small groups of curious people from each of these six cities, not interacting much with those from another city than their own, ventured to the ground of the Old Stadium—where the artists, merchants, food-sellers, and performers of the same six nationalities had set up their stalls. Some spectators tried to enter the Sacred Grove to view inside the magnificent Temple of Zeus. But the Spartans had ordered it closed and had placed sentries in front of it to enforce this deviation from custom.

The dignitaries, after resting for two hours, met in the andron of the Ambassador Quarters; it was lined around its edges with couches, each with a low table in front, on which the important men displayed their finest silver and gold dishes. Entertained by musicians and poets recounting the deeds of past Olympic heroes, the dignitaries enjoyed the sumptuous foods served by their attendants; but the dignitaries did not much engage their counterparts except to extend the shallow courtesies and pleasantries due other leaders of state. Around ten in the evening, Lycurgus called an end to the festivities, and everyone retired.

After the opening ceremony, Archidamus spent the rest of the day in the Gymnasium. There he boxed against his toughest fellow Spartans, all of whom he easily dispatched with savage fury, watched by their stoic comrades, who, as the beaten tumbled, carted

their battered shells off to recover under the colonnades. Penthesilea went with her tribe into the hills to the north of the Olympia
compound, where they had camped far away from others. There
the Amazon champion honed her own skills against her sisters,
sporadically picking fights to interrupt the nonstop drunken revelry
induced by the inhuman volumes of red wine they consumed. The
remaining competitors, guided by their trainers, chose far less rigorous means of preparation, instead stretching and shadow-boxing
(in plain view of each other in the courtyard of the Athlete Quarters) before breaking at sunset for their evening meal.

❧

By one in the morning, all the athletes, except two, had retired
to their respective beds to rest for what promised to be a grueling
first day of competition. While the six others slept, Penthesilea
engulfed in raucous calamity with her sisters in the hills; and
Orion, too excited to sleep, sat on the edge of the pool (outside the
Athlete Quarters) with Cadmus and Hipponax (his official trainers), all of them facing the water and the Gymnasium further on.

"Aria is here," blurted Orion, suddenly turning the subject
away from the magnificent stadium as they all dangled their legs in
the healing waters, trying to relax from the day's bedlam. "I saw
her in the crowd today. She was standing right next to Medea."

"You need to stay away from Aria," replied Cadmus, displeased.
Cadmus also had spotted her in the crowd. But hoping that Orion
didn't, he had chosen not to mention it. Orion seemed too pre-

occupied with her during the six months leading up to the games, even if his obsession did not diminish his performance while helping Hipponax train.

"And why is that?" asked Orion, confused. "Aria has done nothing but help us. Why are you so against her?"

"She will just distract you," Cadmus insisted. "You have more important things to focus on than love. Don't waste your energy on her. Winning the games is going to be difficult enough as it is."

"Maybe she can help me win," replied Orion.

Hipponax nodded agreement, just as the two women they were talking about walked up behind the three friends. Aria and Medea had badgered their father to bring them to the games, and Pytheas had reluctantly agreed on condition that they stay close to him. He had brought them up to believe they could do most anything a man could, but there were limits. Olympia, filled with male strangers, was no place for them to wander alone. And Pytheas regretted his decision even at the opening ceremony when he heard his two daughters asking others in the crowd where the athletes were housed. He made them promise not to sneak out at night to visit Orion and Cadmus, to be alone with them when the Eleans might have time to spend. But knowing their independent natures, which resembled his departed wife's, Pytheas was little convinced that Aria and Medea would keep their word. Sure enough, as soon as he began snoring, the sisters slipped out of the tent they all shared in the Athenian section, still alive with activity on the banks of the Alpheus, south of the New Stadium. Then the sisters stole into the deserted grounds of Olympia. At midnight, as always, the Spartans had ordered the stalls in the Old Stadium closed and had cleared the crowds from the complex back to their tents. And, by now, even the nine hundred soldiers had retired to the Gymnasium, their temporary barracks.

"Hello, Cadmus," eagerly blurted blushing Medea, more than a little excited to see him.

The three Eleans whipped their heads around, and Cadmus, far from enthused by the visitors, replied sharply. "What are you doing here? This area is for participants only."

Aria had not expected Cadmus' harsh reception. Orion's best friend had seemed to like her when her family had hosted the three Eleans back in Athens. But now, though surprised and disappointed, she kept her composure to issue a soft yet resolute response. "I am here for Orion."

"I saw you in the crowd today," Orion spewed, stating the obvious, under pressure of the mounting tension between him and Aria, as the three Eleans sprang up to meet the two women.

"I know," replied Aria, opening her eyes wide before blinking and then dipping her head down and away. "I would not miss the games for anything."

"I'm glad you came," Orion replied. "But it isn't wise for two young ladies to wander Olympia alone, especially at this hour."

"I wanted to wish you good luck," Aria replied, leveling her gaze directly into Orion's as she nervously swept her left hand up and pushed her hair behind her ear.

"Thank you," Orion replied calmly, even if inside he was thrilled. "And now that you have, please let us escort you back to the safety of your tent."

Cadmus grabbed Orion by the arm and pulled him aside. "I'm not going."

"Yes, you are," insisted Orion. "I need you to keep Medea busy, so I can talk to Aria."

"What about Hipponax?" Cadmus suggested. "Take him, and leave me here."

"No, you have to come," Orion explained. "She likes you."

"Then Hipponax has to come too," replied Cadmus. "I refuse to be alone with her."

All the way, as the five went through Olympia, Cadmus walked briskly, trying to stay ahead of Medea, who did everything to keep pace while wearing his ear out with chatter. Hipponax was doing his best to walk between the two, trying to act as a buffer so that Cadmus would not lose his already-fraying temper.

Orion and Aria trailed thirty feet behind. The pauses and uncomfortable silences imposed by their overwhelming physical attraction, by the time they reached their destination, had given way to smooth conversation. Now, just like their previous meetings, they related as if they were longtime companions who knew each other their whole lives.

"He has finally met his match," Orion commented, smiling at the building commotion as Cadmus told Medea what he really thought of her *big mouth!*

"She can be a little overbearing, but she has a heart of gold," replied Aria, not apologizing for her sister, just explaining.

"It seems you both do," said Orion, seriously. "Your father

raised you well."

"Thank you," whispered Aria, further drawn by Orion's gentle sincerity. He had shown the same qualities when she confided her mother's fate, the first night he visited her home in Athens.

Cadmus and Medea erupted into a full-scale argument, both pushing past Hipponax to confront the other, leaving the giant looking on from the sidelines, shaking his big, shaggy head.

Everyone else occupied, Orion, feeling at ease with Aria, took the opportunity to share his deepest fears, hoping that she would not judge him. If Aria could accept him as he was, with all his weaknesses, then her support would mean everything. "I've never faced anyone as tough as the other athletes in this competition. I think I've outlived my usefulness."

"You have just as much chance of winning as they do," insisted Aria, tenderly bolstering Orion in his moment of doubt. "Look at all you have done already. We would not even have these games if not for you."

Aria took a silver chain from around her neck; it had a little gold barn-owl hanging on it. Then she slipped the chain over Orion's head, down around his neck, a far snugger fit.

"What's this?" he asked.

"For good luck," she replied, gently squeezing his hand. "It was given to me by my mother. I have worn it almost my whole life. Now I want you to have it."

Orion looked down at the medallion. He was touched and overwhelmed that Aria, for him, would part with something so dear. "I can't accept this."

Then Aria took Orion's face in her hands. "Look at me. I believe in you. Orion, you are a champion!"

Chapter Ten

LEATHER IN THE FACE

A distant cheer woke Orion around eight the next morning. Instantly sensing he had overslept, he jumped from his bed and rushed out of his room. The Athlete Quarters' colonnades and training area were deserted.

Panic taking hold, Orion ran to the room shared by his official trainers, directly across the courtyard. He burst in, startling Cadmus and Hipponax awake. "We overslept! The others have already left!"

Cadmus and Hipponax rolled out of their beds. Then the three friends bolted out of the room and exited the Athlete Quarters. The pathway and grass outside the building were deserted. The crowd that usually waited there to glimpse the competitors close up had already swept away to the stadium.

Orion and Cadmus, leaving puffing Hipponax running as best

he could behind, raced to the arena, desperately hoping that Orion would arrive in time to compete. And their panic grew as the outside of the bowl came into view. Everyone already had packed inside.

Orion and Cadmus reached the entrance tunnel. As they raced down its dark length, pulses pounding and mouths dry with antici-pation, a loud cheer came from inside the bowl; it vibrated the arch above their heads and sent a shock wave through the passageway that surged the crowd's energy into their bodies.

The noise subsided just as Orion and Cadmus reached the far mouth of the tunnel and stopped inside it, on the edge of the arena floor. Spartan sentries still guarded the perimeter of the competi-tion area. Lycurgus and the Hellanodikes occupied nine of the ten seats of the row of chairs to the right; the two remaining Hellano-dikes stood at the sides of the same row of chairs. The ten ambassa-dors (two trumpeters standing at the sides of their row) occupied the seats directly across the whole width, on the left side of the grass oval. The terraces were filled with spectators, still sitting among their own kind. However, except for the Amazons, now, where their sections met, many among the crowd seemed to briefly acknowledge and converse with those from other cities rather than completely avoiding contact as they had before.

At the center of the arena grass, there was a boxing ring with four wooden corner posts connected by three coarse, fawn-colored ropes. Fifteen people—athletes and trainers—stood around the boxing ring. Meanwhile, the referee, Eurydamos, tall and strong, still an impressive physical specimen though in his waning years, stood inside the ring reviewing the rules. "This is a single-elimination competition. Winners move on to the next round. Losers are out. Three rounds of three minutes each by the water clock. If there is no knockout, the Hellanodikes decide."

Orion and Cadmus strode out of the tunnel to the boxing ring. The crowd exploded with excitement, prompting everyone in and around the ring to stop what they were doing and turn to face the arriving Eleans.

"You're late," snapped Eurydamos, just as Orion and Cadmus reached the boxing ring. In his youth, the referee was Thebes' finest pugilist, retiring unbeaten from competition, crowned Olympic Boxing Champion four times. Once, when another fighter knocked out his front teeth, he swallowed them to avoid seeming hurt and thereby earned the judges' decision.

Now Eurydamos leaned over the ropes and slapped a pair of gloves into Orion's hands—thin rawhide thongs with hard knuckle pads on the outside, designed to cause damage to opponents while protecting a fighter's fists. "Put these on. We've already drawn the lots. You fight first."

Cadmus pulled the gloves on Orion, and he slipped through the ropes just as Hipponax arrived. Meanwhile, Herak of Thebes, bullish redhead with Nordic blood, largest of all the competitors, having donned his pair of hard leather and entered the ring, loomed confidently in the opposite corner, almost half a foot taller and perhaps two wider than Orion.

"Box," shouted Eurydamos, backing out of the center of the ring as Orion and Herak, guards raised, both advanced slowly towards each other.

They met in the middle of the square. Herak swung first. The wide, looping blow with his right fist smashed flush into Orion's face, sending the Elean tumbling into a heap on the ground. Normally, Orion would have eluded such a slow punch, delivered with such poor technique. But he lacked his usual concentration. He had rushed to the stadium without eating or drinking anything, and he had not yet regained his composure, having been suddenly thrust into combat after the panic of arriving almost too late to compete.

"One," shouted Eurydamos, taking up the count. "Two. Three."

Blinking and groggy, Orion got up to his feet.

Herak lumbered in for the kill. He had not expected that Orion, clearly athletic, would be so easy to hit with his powerful but slow punches, delivered with loping swings. And now he was confident of victory.

Orion, fully focusing his attention as best he could through the daze, dodged Herak's blows and stumbled away, buying time to clear his head.

Again, Herak lumbered in to press the attack. But once more, Orion evaded his wide, telegraphed punches, this time dancing away to the other side of the ring.

Herak moved in a third time, swinging away without success, frustrated that he could no longer find his mark. The Theban may have been strong, but he was in no condition to expend so much energy without it taking a drastic toll. With each lunge, he tired more from the effort, and his punches got slower and easier for Orion to evade.

Orion went on the attack, countering Herak's increasingly weary swings with sharp, powerful punches. Now Herak, still unable to hit the young Elean, was taking a beating, yet he kept on coming, swinging and missing, until Orion felled him like a giant tree trunk. Once down, it was clear he was done, and Eurydamos waved the fight off. "That's it. It's over."

Cadmus and Hipponax, who were waiting outside Orion's corner, ran into the ring to congratulate him. In the Athenian section of the stadium crowd, Aria sighed with relief, and Pytheas and Medea celebrated.

❧

Demosthenes and catlike Penthesilea of the Amazons were next, stepping into the ring to face each other for the first time, bearing the rivalry of their entire civilizations in their gloved fists. Athenian and Amazon alike were more animated than other groups in the stadium, the former shouting encouragement to their champion and the latter emitting a combination of shrieks and hisses.

"Box," said Eurydamos, and the fight began with the snarling Penthesilea running across the ring to launch a wild attack, nonstop flurries from all angles. Demosthenes (like Orion, a classic boxer) evaded her animal-like lunges, countering when he could. But she was quick and strong and so unpredictable that her gloves found Demosthenes' face quite a few times before the end of the first round.

"Box," shouted Eurydamos, and the second round began.

Again the Amazon rushed across the ring. But this time, Demosthenes, having solved the puzzle presented by her style, stepped
forward at just the right time to land a crisp, precise left-right
combination to her jaw that dropped her. The Amazon's blows,
coming fast from all angles, may have been unpredictable, but how
she approached to deliver them was not. She always rushed her
long, tan body forward at the same pace, leaving her exposed to a
well-timed counter.

"One," Eurydamos shouted, taking up the count. "Two."

Penthesilea popped up to her feet snarling.

"Box," said Eurydamos.

Again Penthesilea rushed wildly in at Demosthenes, and he
dropped her with another precision one-two to the face. "One,"
shouted Eurydamos. "Two."

Again Penthesilea popped up and rushed in to resume her
savage attack, and again Demosthenes dropped her with one of his
precision combinations.

"It's over," shouted Eurydamos, waving off the fight. Penthesilea rose and started towards Demosthenes.

"That's it," commanded Eurydamos, assertively stepping in her
way to block her from reaching the Athenian, who had raised his
gloves to defend. "That's three knockdowns. You're done." If any
fighter managed to tumble his opponent on this many occasions in
a single round, it counted as a knockout.

Penthesilea, baring her teeth, growled at Eurydamos like a rabid
dog. In the terraces, the Amazons hissed, and the rest of the crowd
cheered, Athenians loudest of all.

❧

Memnon, the stocky Ethiopian warrior representing Mantinea, competed against tall Konon, the quarry worker from Corinth.

"Box," Eurydamos instructed, and the fight began with Memnon and Konon circling each other at center-ring.

Konon stepped in and delivered a powerful right-handed punch, square to the middle of Memnon's chest. But to Konon's surprise, the same gnarled, stone-crushing fist that usually crumbled opponents with a single shot did not seem to have the least bit of impact on the Ethiopian.

The two athletes were still circling each other at center-ring, and Konon struck again with his powerful right hand, this time flush to Memnon's face.

This blow, though it did draw a visible response from the African, carried far from the desired result. Instead of falling, Memnon simply shook his head twice to clear it.

Konon, shocked that Memnon had easily shaken off his best, backed away, scared, as it dawned on him that, for the first time, he would have to accept punishment as well as dish it out. He had never been in a match where an opponent could withstand his power to fight back.

Memnon advanced slowly on his retreating adversary, trapping him in a corner. Now, with the coarse ropes scratching at his back, Konon experienced the terror felt by his own victims in previous fights. The expressionless African bull was a skilled assassin who would show no mercy.

Memnon saw the growing fear on Konon's face. He had witnessed this look before from other opponents. The Ethiopian knew this was a beaten shell of a man trembling before him, and instantly he swarmed in with an overwhelming fury of spiteful punches. The cowering Corinthian champion, arms raised in a feeble attempt to shield, did not even try to respond with blows of his own. Within seconds, a devastating overhand right, the fourteenth shot, knocked him cold. He crumbled to the floor.

❧

Small and speedy Argive peppered Archidamus with a blinding-fast flurry of punches from all angles to open their contest. The mammoth Spartan didn't even have time to react before the teacher from Argos backed away to the other side of the ring, out of his range.

"Stand and fight like a man," shouted Archidamus, pride stinging more than his body as he moved towards Argive, cutting off the ring. Argive was quick, but his punches carried insufficient weight to bother the far sturdier king.

Archidamus cornered Argive. But again the smaller man peppered the larger with a blinding-fast combination, then slipped away under his swing and retreated to the opposite corner. There Argive waited, grinning with confidence.

Archidamus was furious as he turned and followed. Argive was making him look like a buffoon. Now Archidamus cornered Argive again, and the smaller man let fly with another flurry. But this time the larger man, frustration and determination surging energy through his muscles, employed an illegal wrestling move to trap Argive's right arm and then break it. The sound of it snapping reached the top of the terraces. Instantly, Argive dropped to the ground, screaming and writhing in unbearable pain as his trainer rushed into the ring to attend him.

Archidamus raised both gloved fists high above his head in victory, strutting pompously around the ring, serenaded by a chorus of boos from the stadium crowd.

Eurydamos, disgusted, came towards him. "You're disqualified!"

Archidamus, puffing himself up to intimidate, turned to Eurydamos. "What do you mean?" The Spartan kings had chosen Eurydamos for referee because he was, in his day, a brutal competitor, and the kings believed that he would not restrain Archidamus, whose aggression always stretched the bounds of fair play and often overstepped them. But the Spartan kings had forgotten that Eurydamos always had fought within the rules. And they had not counted on his pure love for the sport and his absolute contempt for those who disrespected the discipline on which it was based.

Now Eurydamos, expanding his own chest to meet the far younger man's challenge, held fast to his decision. "You know what I mean. You're out of the boxing competition."

"We'll see about that!" Archidamus replied sarcastically. Then, with the palms of both rawhide-wrapped hands, he pushed Eurydamos hard in the chest, trying to knock him back.

To the Spartan king's surprise, the old boxer did not budge

even half a step; instead, he stood strong and unyielding. "Get out of the ring, Archidamus. It's time for the next fight."

❦

Orion and Demosthenes, having won their previous contests, faced each other in the first semifinal bout, which was more notable for artistry than savagery. Both men held the other in such high regard that it could hardly be said a single blow was thrown in anger. And by the end of the three rounds, the spectators had been treated to a noble, tactical contest between two master boxers who practiced the sweet science to perfection.

"Well done, Demosthenes," said Orion, sportingly.

"Thank you," replied the Athenian general, graciously, "and you too."

"Good fight, gentlemen," said Eurydamos, with sincere appreciation. "It's up to the judges now."

Orion and Demosthenes, each having pulled off his right glove, shook hands.

In the Athenian section of the stadium crowd, Pytheas reassured Aria as she waited nervously, fingers crossed. "I think Orion did slightly better than Demosthenes."

"But you never know," added Medea, trying to keep Aria from getting her hopes up too much. Boxing judges were notorious for rendering decisions in absolute contradiction to what everyone else had seen with their own eyes.

Moments later, the Chief Hellanodike, Solorchus, sitting next to Lycurgus, acting on the king's instruction or in keeping with his oath to judge fairly, whispered the decision to the flamboyant Elean announcer. Then, everyone in the stadium tense with anticipation, Ibycus strode from arena-edge all the way into the ring. Once more at the center of the drama—his gestures, body gyrations, and voice fluctuations were as entertaining as ever. "After such a noble contest, it is only fitting that our esteemed judges decide the outcome. And they have. The winner, by a single point, is Orion of Elis!"

Eurydamos raised Orion's hand in victory, and the entire crowd applauded, Aria loudest of all. The Amazons had stormed out of the stadium after Penthesilea lost. Every other group that remained in the terraces bore goodwill to the young Elean for his role in reviving the games, and now that he had accomplished what few believed possible—defeating renowned Demosthenes—they eagerly showered him with heartfelt admiration.

❧

The second semifinal featured Memnon against Argive, who earlier had won by disqualification over his Spartan opponent. Archidamus had protested to the judges, trying to overturn the result. But the Spartans, confident at having chosen a referee to suit their needs perfectly, before the competition began, specifically had ordained that his decision would be final. Archidamus would not be reinstated, even if Argive was too injured to compete.

Argive, his broken right arm strapped tightly to his body with a white cloth, was indeed in no condition to box. Nevertheless, refusing to withdraw while he still had even the slightest chance of winning, he chose to step into the ring. If he could use his left hand to build up points and call on his nimble legs to stay away from powerful Memnon, then he might be able to last to the end and gain the judges' favor.

"Box," commanded Eurydamos, and the match began.

The muscular African bull moved purposefully towards the other corner, where the slightly shorter and much leaner man waited, almost fifty pounds lighter than him.

But as Memnon arrived, Argive, with his left hand, landed a series of light blows (barely more hard than taps) to the Ethiopian's head and then escaped with his speedy feet to the other side of the ring.

Memnon pursued. And again as the African arrived, Argive dealt a rapid-fire flurry of glancing touches to his head, and then escaped, practically running, to the other side of the ring.

This time the African bull closed to finish, swarming through the light shots skating off his forehead to launch a vicious attack that dazed the one-armed fighter, leaving him leaning up against the ropes, defenseless.

Now Memnon pulled back his gloved right hand and delivered a hammer-strike to the top of Argive's head, near the temple. It knocked the teacher's consciousness into oblivion and his body out of the ring through the cords.

Orion, standing with the other athletes, looking on from just outside the ropes, was shocked by the cold brutality of the man he would face next. The Ethiopian could easily have dispatched his victim in far less savage fashion. His choice to do otherwise had left Argive littered on the arena grass, while Argive's trainer, aided by others, desperately tried in vain to revive him.

❦

Twenty minutes later, Orion and Memnon (glaring threateningly at him) stood two feet from each other at center-ring, separated by Eurydamos between them. Ibycus, standing a foot behind the referee, projected his voice into the terraces. "All other competitors have been eliminated. Now, these two men face each other in a winner-take-all final bout to decide which of them will become the Olympic Boxing Champion."

"Touch gloves," the referee instructed the fighters.

Orion stuck out his gloves waist-high in front of himself, expecting that Memnon would do the same to gently tap the front of his own gloves to Orion's in the customary salute between finalists. Instead, Memnon slammed his gloves hard down on top of Orion's.

Then the two pugilists turned and went back to their respective corners on opposite sides. Eurydamos held at center-ring; Ibycus exited through the ropes, right next to Cadmus and Hipponax, standing just outside Orion's corner.

"Box," shouted Eurydamos, and the African bull raced across the grass of the roped square directly at Orion, who stepped forward to meet him.

Memnon, far stronger than Orion, though two inches shorter,

dealt out a relentless body attack. Orion, unable to counter with anything that came close to discouraging the vicious assault, just absorbed punishment. Each crunching blow to his ribs shook him through to the spine.

Memnon's first punch to the head, an overhand right, landed above Orion's left temple, putting him down instantly. It felt like he had been hit by a rock.

"One," Eurydamos began; Orion, head spinning and vision blurred, rolled on the grass, struggling to find the ground beneath his feet before the referee arrived at ten. "Two. Three. Four."

In the moment that Eurydamos sounded five, Orion, with every ounce of strength, rose to one knee. Then at six, still woozy, he shot up to his feet, knowing that to survive he must stay away from the Ethiopian until the cobwebs cleared their tangle from around his brain. Otherwise, like Argive, he could end up strewn on the arena floor, clinging to life by a thread.

"Box," Eurydamos commanded, and Memnon swarmed in to finish.

Now Orion used his skill, slipping punches to avoid the worst of the assault. But then Memnon caught the young Elean on the head with another overhand right, again sending him sprawling to the ground. There he lay face-down on the grass, motionless.

"One," counted Eurydamos, as Orion, shaking his head to clear the cobwebs, tried to rise. "Two. Three."

Then Orion pushed his arms against the ground, lifting himself to one knee. Though the second blow to the head had been as strong as the first, its terrible impact having been felt once before, it did not come as such a shock, and this time Orion was able to recover from it faster.

Now, to everyone in the stadium, Orion's body looked fresh enough that he could reclaim his feet. But he did not, and his face told why. He didn't want to fight anymore. He was afraid. He would stay down and let the referee count him out.

"Four," continued Eurydamos. "Five."

"Come on, Orion," Aria mouthed to herself in the Athenian section of the crowd. "Get up." She still believed he could win.

"Six," continued the referee. "Seven."

"Get up, Orion," shouted Hipponax, from just outside the ropes, as Eurydamos reached eight. "Get up!"

"Nine," shouted Eurydamos, emphatically warning Orion that this was his last chance as the young Elean stared across the ring at powerful Memnon, banging his gloves together, eager to destroy.

Suddenly, Orion sprang up to standing, just as Eurydamos' lips began moving to say ten. But, no sound yet emitted, the referee halted them.

Orion remained exactly where he had risen. His legs were weak. They would not carry him well. Win or lose—this was the spot where he must make his stand.

Memnon moved in. The taste of another kill alive in his mouth, he began beating on Orion's body. Yet somehow, Orion was able to weather the storm for the ten seconds before the trumpets sounded and Eurydamos pulled Memnon off. "The round's over, back to your corners."

"How are you feeling?" asked Hipponax, who had come into

the ring to help Orion back to his stool, placed in the corner by Cadmus.

"I'm okay," replied Orion, sitting down on the stool, frustrated.

Cadmus poured refreshing water over his fighter's head as a million thoughts spun around inside of it.

"He's throwing too many punches and hitting too hard, and I can't hurt him to keep him off," Orion continued. "I don't know how much longer I can last."

"Okay, take it easy," said Cadmus, sensing that Orion's frustration was growing to fluster. "Here's what you do. When he throws the overhand right, he drops his left. Just step in a little to your right and come up underneath with an uppercut." Cadmus, in addition to having boxed as a youth, had observed Orion fight many times, and now he was a master strategist who could spot even the slightest weakness in any opponent's style.

Hipponax and Cadmus (with the stool) exited the ring, and Orion stood to face Memnon, already on his feet in the other corner, ready to charge.

Then Eurydamos gave the order, "Box!"

"Okay," Cadmus instructed from just outside the ropes. "Go get him. And remember what I told you."

Memnon raced across the ring, Orion stepped forward to meet him, and both landed powerful blows to the other's chest. However, the result could not have been more different. Memnon was as unaffected as if a fly had landed on him; Orion was knocked back into the wooden corner post behind.

Now Memnon resumed his vicious attack on Orion's body, and then, sensing that his opponent was ready to fall, he threw an overhand right to Orion's temple. Orion, exactly as instructed by Cadmus, with picture-perfect precision, evaded it and rocked Memnon with a powerful right uppercut to the bottom of the chin, snapping his head up and back.

No fighter had ever hurt Memnon like this, and the African bull, in anger, immediately threw another overhand right to Orion's head.

But Orion countered with another perfect uppercut to the bottom of Memnon's chin, more devastating than the last. The Ethiopian wobbled back with a shocked look on his face. His eyes glazed over. Then he tumbled forward, face-first into the ground. And there he lay, immobile.

Orion waited, hoping that Memnon would not rise, as Eurydamos took up the count. "One. Two. Three. Four. Five. Six. Seven. Eight. Nine. Ten! You're out!"

Chapter Eleven

THE PLOT THICKENS

Minutes later, the African bull having been revived, Lycurgus, attended by five Spartan soldiers, stood at the center of the boxing ring, placing a garland of olive leaves on Orion's head to crown him champion of the first event. The terraces exploded with applause. Orion, in addition to restoring the games, had won the crowd's respect and admiration with his valiant performance, regardless of affiliation with any city.

Competition over for the day, everyone streamed out of the stadium. After their customary rest, the dignitaries resumed their formal pleasantries in the Ambassador Quarters' andron until eleven at night, when each adjourned once more to his private room. The spectators from the six cities (no Amazons or Spartans), unlike previous days when they mostly remained in their own areas with their own kind, now flooded towards the common ground of the Old Stadium. And more than before they interacted with those from other places than their own cities as they browsed the merchant stalls, enjoyed colorful performances, and even spoke about the day's competition. Then at midnight, as usual, the Spartans ordered an end to activity on the common ground of the Old Stadium. The merchants and performers closed their stalls, and the spectators all returned to their separate tent districts, where they feasted until the early morning, once more divided by nationality.

The Amazons, who had returned to their camp in the hills immediately after their entrant was eliminated from boxing, continued their rowdy ways through the rest of the day until nine at night. Then Penthesilea informed her sisters that she was leaving to take up residence in the Athlete Quarters. The other Amazons were surprised. It was Amazon custom that all warriors engage in revelry with the rest of the tribe by night, especially when they were engaged in battle by day. But they acceded when she insisted forcefully, despite pressure from her peers to the contrary, that she break with their accustomed ways. She blamed a lack of sleep from the previous night's festivities for her inability to defeat Demosthenes. Now Penthesilea, knowing that she could rest better in her assigned lodging, would not let anything stand in the way of her winning the games, even the strain of parting with her sisterhood's common mode.

Argive, after being dispatched by Memnon, had been revived and carried by the finest physicians of Argos to his room. There he screamed as the doctors tried over and over to reset the bones in his broken right arm. Two hours later they finally succeeded. Then the doctors wrapped it tight in layers of white cloth to hold it firm, and soon after that, exhausted, the teacher went to sleep.

After leaving the stadium, Orion, Demosthenes, Memnon, Konon, and Herak went immediately into their own rooms to eat a huge meal and then lay down to rest. Each of them intended to stay in bed until early the next morning—then rise recovered from the brutal first event and fully ready for the next dangerous competition. Archidamus, however, did not rest. He and his fellow Spartan king had matters to attend.

❧

About two hours after midnight, a contingent of twenty Spartans, led by their harsh captain, slipped swiftly and silently through the door into Konon's room in the Athlete Quarters. Konon woke to find a sword at his throat and a hand over his mouth.

"Come quietly," instructed the captain, "and no harm will fall on you."

Realizing he had little choice, Konon got up from his bed, and the Spartans led him out of his room, all the way to the Temple of Zeus. Then, in the same manner, the twenty Spartans returned five more times to the Athlete Quarters to gather, one by one, from their rooms, each of the remaining athletes bedded there, except Orion.

Demosthenes was last of the six herded towards the massive Temple of Zeus. As he entered the Sacred Grove, he saw that the outside of the bright-white building, enveloped in darkness, was deserted. And it remained quiet even as the Spartans marched him up the steps, between the columns, and towards the closed solid-bronze door.

Demosthenes stopped as he reached the entrance, reluctant to go further, wondering what the armed men standing behind him intended to do. Could he trust their assurances that no harm would come to him—or were they leading him to his death?

"Get in there," ordered the Spartan captain, pushing the Athenian general in the back.

Demosthenes opened the right side of the door and walked through the entrance, followed by the captain, who pulled the portal shut behind. Torches lit the inside of the long and high hall; its open floor, lined by tall columns, was dominated by the solemn-ly majestic statue of Zeus, sitting two hundred feet away from the entrance at the far end. Fashioned by the sculptor Phidias, the same man who was so instrumental in building the Parthenon on Athens' Acropolis, the statue was widely regarded as one of the Seven Wonders of the World. The god, forty-three feet tall as he sat, had his flesh made in pristine ivory. His cloak, sandals, and elaborate throne were made of rich gold. In his open right palm, he held a life-sized statue of Nike, also made of pure rich yellow and ivory. And in his left hand, he held a scepter of precious metals, with a golden eagle, almost as large as Nike, at its top.

The two Spartan kings (attended by twenty more armed troops) stood a yard in front of the magnificent statue, facing Demosthenes at the entrance and the other five summoned athletes. They stood ten yards away from Lycurgus and Archidamus on the temple's open floor, looking at the monarchs and Zeus on his throne behind.

"Demosthenes," greeted Archidamus. "We have been waiting for you. Come forward so we can begin the business at hand."

"Get on with it, Archidamus," snarled Penthesilea. "Why have we been brought here?"

"Yes, Archidamus," Demosthenes added as he walked forward to join the other athletes, "why have we been brought here? And where is Orion?"

"Two very good questions," said Lycurgus, taking over from his younger counterpart. "If Orion wins the chariot race tomorrow, then he becomes the Olympic Grand Champion, thereby denying that honor to you all. It is in everyone's interest to make sure that does not happen."

"Corinth does not cheat," emphatically replied Konon, with no regard for his city's alliance with the Spartans outside Olympia.

"Neither does Athens," added Demosthenes. "Such a conspiracy defies the spirit of the Olympic Games. I will not dishonor myself or this sacred competition."

"Your sentiments are noble but clearly misguided," said Lycurgus, resorting to cunning in the face of resistance. "Allowing the simpleton sheepherder to win would bring more shame to the Olympic Games than if we merely arranged matters to ensure a champion worthy of the mantle. Must I remind you that the person who rises to Olympic Grand Champion will instantly become a hero to all of Greece? Dare we allow such influence to fall to someone who would not wield it in a fitting manner?"

"I don't care what Greece thinks of me," snarled Penthesilea.

"But I will join you. I came to win."

"I, too, will do my part," said Memnon. "I have traveled the world, scratching and clawing for victory. I don't surrender it to anyone."

"And where do the two of you stand?" Lycurgus said, turning to Herak and Argive. "Can we count on you?"

Both athletes stayed silent, refusing to take a position despite more prodding from Lycurgus.

"A word of caution to those who will not join us," said Archidamus, after ten more minutes of discussion had failed to produce a different vote from anyone. "Be warned. Do not get in our way, lest you also suffer a terrible accident tomorrow."

❧

Orion, unable to sleep any more, had woken fifteen minutes before the Spartans came for the first of the other athletes whom they whisked away to the Temple of Zeus. Hipponax and Cadmus, though having not long put their heads down, were already dreaming in their own room. So Orion, unaware of the conspiracy at hand, stole out of the Athlete Quarters alone and crossed the deserted Olympia complex to the Athenian section of tents, still alive with activity. There Orion found Aria, and she walked and talked with him even as the Spartans were waking Konon with a sword held to his throat and a hand over his mouth.

"I hope your father wasn't angry that I took you away from his tent at this late hour," Orion said.

"Are you serious?" Aria responded, smiling at how much her father liked and approved of Orion. "He couldn't shove me out fast enough."

"Nevertheless," Orion explained, "I didn't mean to be rude, just showing up like I did and asking you to go for a walk with me. I just really need to talk to you."

Aria looked at Orion, concerned by his pensive demeanor. "About?"

"I want to thank you for giving me the courage to win today," said Orion, looking right at her.

Aria seemed confused.

"When Memnon had me down the second time, I was scared," explained Orion, breaking their gaze to look down at the ground, embarrassed. "I wanted to quit. That's never happened to me before."

Orion drew his eyes up from the ground to meet Aria's again. "Then, just as the referee was about to count me out, I thought about how much you believe in me, and suddenly that was the only thing that mattered. I wasn't afraid any more. And I guess the rest is history."

"I'm glad I could help," replied Aria, tears welling in her eyes. She was truly moved that her connection to Orion had the power to inspire him in his darkest hour, yet she also was deeply pained that her hero had experienced enough terror to shake his resolve.

Now Aria kissed Orion, and he responded. Each had waited for this moment since the day they met in Athens' Agora, hopefully wondering if it would ever come. And as anticipation became reality, with lips pressed together for the first time, both could feel the other's trembling energy flowing into their own bodies.

❧

The Spartan army had arrived outside Athens that afternoon and had finished setting up their camp of crimson tents over the same ground where they had rested eight months before, outside the range of the skilled Scythian archers atop Athens' ramparts. And while Orion walked with Aria, the soldiers of the blood-red and shining bronze, wasting no time, turned their attention to priming for battle. Some calmly groomed their plaited hair. Some checked the leather bindings on their armor. Some polished the faces of their shields. Others filed their gleaming weapons to utmost sharpness.

And as each Spartan prepared, his thoughts were one with his comrades. He looked forward to inflicting as much suffering as he could on the hated enemy who had wounded his honor the last time he was here. Perhaps it was General Brasidas who said it best as he stood at the edge of the Spartan camp, next to the massive wooden objects (still under white cloths), looking towards Athens' walls (aglow with torches and filled with defenders). "Tomorrow, hell begins."

Chapter Twelve

THE CHARIOT RACE

T he next morning, Orion arrived at the stadium well in time for the start of the much-anticipated chariot race, perhaps the most thrilling of all Olympic sports. And as he waited for the event to be announced, he stood silently next to the other athletes at the center of the arena in the space vacated by the removed boxing ring. Each was a bundle of nervous energy, scanning the surroundings.

Though the stadium crowd still sat mostly divided by affiliation, now some spectators of other nationalities were intermingled in the sections that previously had been uniformly composed of people from one place. The Amazons, however, still keeping to themselves, formed a notable exception to this fresh distribution.

Lycurgus, sterner than before, sat among the men wearing purple robes in the center of the row of ornate chairs on the right

side of the grass, directly across from the row of ambassadors. As on the two previous days, armed Spartans stood sentry all around the arena floor, their faces stone cold as ever.

A round, thick, seven-foot-high wooden stake had been planted in the floor, thirty yards in front of the end of the arena that lay furthest from the stadium tunnel. A garland of olive leaves rested atop it. Eight wooden chariots—flimsy two-wheeled carriages that were harnessed to four massive horses—were lined up next to each other; they were even with the stake—four on either side of it—and they faced the narrow stadium exit at the distant end of the bowl.

"Welcome to the greatest test of speed known to man," Ibycus announced, standing next to the athletes as flamboyant as ever. "Today, these fearless competitors will race over the most challenging course in the history of the Olympic Games. They must exit the stadium, travel through Olympia, cross the bridge at her southwestern side, pass the short flat, wind through the wooded hills, and then burst onto the plain. Once there, they must cross another river by bridge, round the Giant Cypress Tree, and return by the same route. The winner will be the one that first enters the stadium and gathers the garland from atop the pole."

Now the athletes walked over and mounted the chariots, which they had already chosen by drawing lots. Demosthenes' chariot, powered by four white stallions, sat to the immediate right of the chariot selected by Orion. And as the racers readied for the start, the Athenian general looked over at the young Elean, whose black leather reins were wrapped tight around his hands, ready to urge his four chestnuts forward. "Be careful, Orion. Some will resort to unfair means to deny you victory."

Archidamus had selected the carriage powered by four jet-black steeds, to the immediate left of Orion. And now the Spartan king cast an evil eye at the Athenian general.

"Ready," shouted Ibycus. "Steady. Go!"

The entire crowd surged to its feet in a single wave of energy as the horses lurched forward, beginning the powerful rush across the length of the arena towards the exit at the other end.

The narrow tunnel was wide enough for only one cart to pass at a time. As they neared it, the racers maneuvered and jostled for position. In the confusion, Argive (riding the chariot on the extreme left of the pack, injured right arm tied to his body) was unable to keep control. His carriage toppled over on top of him, instantly snapping his neck.

Meanwhile, at the front, Orion squeaked into the tunnel in the lead—followed in order by Herak, Penthesilea, Memnon, Archidamus, Demosthenes, and Konon.

Soon after, having stormed through the channel, the chariots flew out the other end of the entranceway. Now the great number of spectators lining the path outside watched with great excitement as the mighty horses, sweeping their cargo along, thundered past just a few feet in front of them and then continued on down towards the slender wooden bridge at Olympia's southwest corner.

The distance there was too short and the path in between the crowd was not wide enough to overtake, and thus the order of the chariots remained the same as the racers flew up to and rattled across the platform. Without a change in array, they stormed past the short, shrubby flat and started into the narrow course that snaked through the wooded hills. Here too—along the slender, winding, undulating, tree-lined route—it would be difficult to pass. But that did not stop some, especially Penthesilea, from trying, and there were many near crashes. Still, no racer was able to overhaul another.

Thus, as they stormed down from the hills onto the broad plain, the chariots were in the same sequence as when they had left the stadium. Now the racers were free to spread out, but they still bunched together in somewhat of a tight pack; those who followed were drafting behind the leaders so that their horses could keep pace without expending as much energy.

Then, at the front of the pack, Herak (the ginger-haired Theban whom Orion had felled like a giant tree trunk) pulled next to Orion and rammed his chariot hard into the Elean's, trying to overturn it. But Orion kept control of his skating cart. Again, Herak pulled next to Orion, and again he tried to ram. This time Orion slowed to dodge the lunge, and Herak missed, his momentum carrying the back of his chariot across in front of Orion's four chestnut horses. Meanwhile, all the other racers moved wide around to pass the embattled two.

Konon, the quarry worker, looked back from the rear of the passing pack. Herak had renewed his assault on Orion, and though Konon, out of his own desire for victory, tried to leave matters alone, he could not let this injustice pass. Now he slowed his chariot alongside Herak, wedging the man from Thebes between himself and Orion. Then he swerved his chariot into Herak's, causing them both to capsize; their tumbling carts barely missed the back of Orion's wheels.

Now Orion looked ahead. At the front of the pack, some forty yards away, Penthesilea raced into the lead—followed by Archidamus, Demosthenes, and Memnon.

Determined to recover the distance, the young Elean drove his horses hard, and soon enough he pulled within ten yards of Memnon, still at the rear of the group.

Now Memnon looked back and saw Orion, and his expression hardened. Then, without warning, the Ethiopian warrior drew out a dagger, previously hidden within his vessel's walls, and flung it back.

Orion's eyes grew large as he saw the short, thick blade tumbling end-over-end through the air, directly towards his face.

He ducked. The dagger hummed by, barely missing his left ear. An inch closer—and it would not have.

Orion looked up ahead again as the chariots approached the second wooden bridge. It would carry them across the river to the Giant Cypress Tree, standing alone, a hundred yards further, on the other side of the grassy flat.

But the African bull had not exhausted his stash of hidden weapons, and he cast another dagger back through the air. It tumbled at Orion but missed low. With a thud, it pierced the front wall of the Elean's cart, right in front of him.

Now the crossing was upon them. The racers, one at a time, guided their chariots onto the narrow bridge—Penthesilea, Archidamus, Demosthenes, Memnon, and then Orion. Its timbers, never meant to carry such weight, creaked and strained under the collective force as the horses pounded along towards the other side, dragging the rattling carts fast behind.

Bursting from the bridge onto the flat, the racers drove towards the Giant Cypress Tree. Penthesilea, quickly eclipsing the hundred yards, reached first, but as she rounded the trunk, having not slowed enough, her speed carried her wide around.

Archidamus, cutting the turn fine and almost capsizing, seized the lead from her on the inside. Demosthenes, catching the same line as the Spartan king, followed. Penthesilea, able to regain control, swerved in front of Memnon as the African rounded with Orion biting at his heels.

Now as the chariots hurtled back towards the first bridge for the return journey, Memnon drew another piece of sharp-bladed cargo from within the front wall of his cart. This time, resolved to aim true, he looked carefully back at Orion, trying to gauge his target, even as the leaders, just in front of him, reached the crossing. Quickly, Memnon released the dagger back into the draft. Then he turned to look forward. But the platform was closer than he had counted on, and he did not have the proper line to steer his chariot on. Instead, it sailed at full speed into midair and then plunged into the water below.

Orion, distracted by having to duck the blade slicing through the slipstream at him, barely skidded his vessel onto the bridge to avoid the same fate as the African.

The four remaining chariots—of Archidamus, Demosthenes, Penthesilea, and Orion—returned across the plain, towards the rolling hills, two miles away. But now, with the horses fatiguing, it was a strategic battle of cat and mouse, and the order changed back and forth as each racer tried to gain position, while at the same time saving some of his steeds' speed for the final push to pass first onto the road snaking through the wooded slopes. After that, there would be no clear-cut opportunity for anyone to overtake the leader along what remained of the course.

The chariots approached within a hundred yards of the hills, and the jockeying for position became more intense, and the speed steadily increased to full. Then, with fifty yards left, Orion pulled wide to the outside and passed the other three, tightly packed as they jostled each other. Fighting off hard challenges, he kept his lead and then cut in to enter the hills first. Archidamus, Penthesilea, and Demosthenes stormed along behind. There was not more than a foot between any of the racers.

In the same order, the chariots hurtled through the narrow, winding, undulating, tree-lined course. Without a change in array, they flew onto and past the flat at the bottom of the hills; then they pounded across the bridge into Olympia, between the gawking spectators packed on both sides of the path that led towards the narrow arena tunnel up ahead.

Suddenly, Archidamus weaved to the right, the crowd on that side scattering out of his way to avoid being trampled. Now the Spartan king drove his horses hard, and his chariot pulled alongside Orion's. The Elean's horses had spent their best at the entrance to the hills, and they were more tired than those that powered his challenger.

"Yah," shouted Orion, flapping the tight-gripped reins as he saw Archidamus' blacks, harnesses jangling and manes flowing in the wind, drawing even with his chestnuts. Now Orion's four stallions, surging with their last burst of energy, began inching ahead again.

As they drew to within forty yards of the stadium entrance, Orion was only half a foot ahead of Archidamus, but the young Elean occupied the line that would allow him to speed directly into the tunnel. The racer who penetrated the stadium at the front would have a practically unassailable advantage.

Archidamus swerved left and crashed his chariot into Orion's, trying to barge him out of the way to take the lead. But Orion (almost sent flying out of his cart by the force of the hit) clung on, righting his charge just as he reached within ten yards of the stadium entrance, still holding superior position.

But Archidamus could not let Orion win and become Olympic Grand Champion, even if that meant sacrificing himself in this event. He swerved his chariot harder into the Elean's. The collision sent men, horses, wood, metal, and leather tumbling, with a thunderous crash, into the outside of the stadium wall to the left of the entrance.

The way now clear, Penthesilea, screaming delighted, raced into the tunnel with Demosthenes in hot pursuit. And soon they both rushed out of the other end of the walled passage into the stadium.

Now the terrace crowd roared and came to its feet as it watched Penthesilea and Demosthenes, frantically urging their tired horses on, race for the garland that sat on the pole at the other end of the arena grass.

The noise increased as Demosthenes catapulted his chariot almost even with the gloating Amazon just as she reached her hand to grasp victory. Then the sound amplified to deafening as Demosthenes, on the other side of the pole, stretched better than Penthesilea—whose bulging eyes had already counted the olive leaves as won—to snatch the garland before her coming fingers could.

Now the two racers pulled their chariots to abrupt stops, avoiding an otherwise sure collision with the scattering Spartan soldiers and the waist-high wall at the rounded end of the stadium grass, thirty yards beyond the wooden victory stake.

Demosthenes, still standing in his cart, turned and defiantly locked eyes with Lycurgus. Then he placed the garland to crown himself champion of the second event, and the terraces, except of course the snarling Amazons, honored the Athenian general with a standing ovation that shook the entire stone structure.

Soon after the applause had died, word of Orion's terrible crash, spreading like wildfire through the crowd, reached Cadmus and Hipponax. Hearts pounding, they left the terraces and rushed out of the stadium.

Spartan soldiers were helping a shaken Archidamus from his crashed chariot. He seemed in remarkably good condition considering that his vehicle had been reduced to little more than a few large pieces of wood. His horses (they took the wall most directly) had suffered the worst of the impact. Two of the four magnificent black stallions already lay dead. One other was in the process of expiring, and the last would have to be put out of its misery an hour later.

Now Archidamus looked over at his adversary, pleased with his handiwork. The young sheepherder had not been as fortunate as the king. Orion's carriage had borne the brunt of the impact; it had been reduced to little more than small pieces of jagged wood tangled up with black leather reins. And Orion now lay unconscious and battered in its splintered remains. Having been spared serious harm, the four chestnuts were being quieted by some of the spectators.

"Orion," Cadmus shouted as he and Hipponax arrived and knelt to attend to their prone friend. Orion looked as pale as Aeneas had looked, when the three of them had found his wolf-eaten body beneath the tree with black bark and bright-red leaves, over seven months ago, in the foggy mountain gorge.

There was no response, and now they noticed that Orion had blood coming from his mouth.

"Orion," said Hipponax, grabbing his hand. "Can you hear me?"

Again, there was no response.

Chapter Thirteen

BESIEGED AND BATTERED

On the same morning that the chariot race was held, just as the racers burst out of the stadium, the five thousand Spartan invaders formed war ranks outside their camp, facing Athens. But, contrary to their habit on previous campaigns, they did not rush in shortly after taking shape for battle. Instead, all day long, like statues, there the storm troopers stood, no man moving a muscle or cracking an expression.

Then as night fell and deepened into full dark, General Brasidas, on his mottled white stallion, arrived in front of the troops and issued the command. "Bring them forward."

The ranks parted down the middle to allow ten large wooden catapults through, no longer shrouded under white cloth. Each massive crossbow (mounted at an angle on a frame supported by four wheels) was pulled with ropes by a hundred soldiers.

Then the gap flowed shut behind the last of the weapons as it passed forward to join its brothers, twenty yards away, in a line drawn flat across the front of the troops.

"Rain terror, Captain," ordered Brasidas, from atop his mount, midway between the back of the row of catapults and the front of the reformed ranks.

"Ready," Terpander commanded. He was standing on the ground next to Brasidas.

The catapult crews drew the massive bowstrings back and down, fastening them in place so that their comrades could load the large stones into the black leather cups at the center of each cord. Three rocks the size of human heads per catapult.

"Fire," Terpander shouted.

One by one, rippling down the whole row from right to left, the catapult cords snapped forward, launching the volley of rocks into the air.

When the Spartan army arrived the day before, General Nicias had ordered the women and children to the Acropolis and rallied the defenders to man the walls. He had since been perplexed that the Spartans (usually eager once formed in battle array) had not yet stormed forward under their blood-red and shining bronze canopy of shields. But he was even more confused that after nightfall the enemy ranks still remained in formation, mostly covered by darkness. They had lit only a few torches, and the two-day-old moon was completely shrouded by strange orange-black clouds.

As the Spartans pulled their catapults forward, young Captain Marathon stood next to Nicias on Athens' well-lit wall, midway between the Dipylon and Sacred Gateways. Both officers looked towards the Spartan army. Its outline barely visible in the distance, they could not see the weapons that were uncovered for the first time since the invaders arrived, and neither was able to determine what the enemy intended.

"What are they doing?" asked Nicias, puzzled.

"I see movement," Marathon replied. "They must finally be getting ready to storm."

"Archers, ready," Nicias commanded.

The corps of Scythians stepped to the front of the wall, placed their feathered arrows, and drew the strings back as they angled their bows upwards and away.

Still the two Athenian officers did not guess the danger, even as the Spartans launched the deadly volley of stones that was now hurtling towards the manned ramparts through the night sky.

Marathon, concerned and puzzled, furrowed his brow. The young captain thought he heard a faint whistling noise. He did not know what was causing it, but he instinctively sensed that something was wrong.

Suddenly, the volley of stones landed, hitting first to the left of where the officers stood, ripping hardest into the front of the wall and the unsuspecting archers at the fore, bows angled up and away, ready to fire.

Then the landing volley of stones rippled along the ramparts from left to right, moving towards Nicias and Marathon.

"Get down," shouted Marathon, warning the others as he ducked behind the chest-high wall at the front of the walkway and pulled Nicias down with him. "Everyone, get down. Take cover."

Many Athenian defenders, understanding Marathon's meaning, followed suit. Yet some of these men were felled by rocks that burst through the foot-deep wall at the very top of the protected walkway. Other defenders, still confused or frozen with panic, did not take cover before the wave of landing rocks, continuing down past the right of the two officers, reached them.

Then the stones stopped coming.

"What should we do, Nicias?" asked Marathon, surveying the terrible toll taken by the Spartans' new weapon of mass destruction. The dead and wounded lay all around, while those who had been spared physical injury, though shocked and terrified, helped those hurt.

Nicias, too shaken to answer, just blankly stared around at the damage.

Marathon, one hand on each of the general's shoulders, grabbed his superior officer and shook him. "Pull yourself together, General! What should we do?"

"We wait behind the cover of our walls," replied Nicias, snapping out of the trance.

"Wait for what?" Marathon shouted. "For the Spartans to bludgeon us to death—twenty at a time? Let me take the men out. A charge is our only hope."

"No, Marathon," sternly commanded Nicias, regaining his full composure to rein in his brash junior officer from pursuing what he regarded as yet another impulsive course. "You stand no chance against them in open ground. A charge is suicide. I won't allow it.

We wait behind the cover of our walls, and that's final, Captain."

Marathon, about to reply with disgust at what he perceived as cowardice, bit his tongue. The young captain had little respect for his cautious superior. But Marathon honored Nicias' rank enough to silence his own voice in the face of a direct order.

Meanwhile, back at the Spartan formation, Brasidas wryly ordered another volley. He could not have been more matter of fact. "Again."

Terpander eagerly gave the order to the catapult crews. "Ready."

Once more the Spartans prepared the giant slingshots to launch.

"Fire," Terpander shouted.

One by one, rippling right to left down the whole row, the ten catapults launched another volley of stones at Athens.

❧

Earlier that day, immediately after the crash, massive Hipponax had lifted Orion's limp, bleeding body from his shattered chariot and carried him quickly from the foot of the stadium wall through crowded Olympia to his room in the Athlete Quarters. Meanwhile, Cadmus, walking at their side, pleaded desperately for a doctor to step forward from among the spectators. But none did, arrogantly certain that the sheepherders could not afford their services, despite Cadmus' promises to the contrary.

Then the finest physician in all of Greece burst into the room just as Hipponax laid Orion gently down on his cot.

"I heard what happened," said Hippocrates. "I came as soon as I could." The tall, thin, graying, seventy-seven-year-old doctor (originally from the island of Cos but now residing in Corinth) had dedicated his whole life to healing others. Long ago, in his early thirties, he had become famous when he established a school where he and his colleagues developed and taught the leading medical procedures known to man, along with the proper ethical principles to guide their implementation. It was the practice in his own life of the most sacred of all these oaths that immediately brought him hurrying to Orion's aid upon learning of the athlete's failing condition and inability to solicit care; no physician should ever stand by and allow suffering when he was in a position to alleviate it, regardless of where the patient came from or if he could pay his healer.

Now Hippocrates set to practicing his art, carefully examining the young man sprawled senseless before him. Orion's muscular frame, which had seemed so powerful less than an hour before as he mounted his ill-fated chariot at the start of the race, had now been reduced to a brittle shell.

Aria, terrified at what she might find, burst frantically into the room, followed by her father and sister. Pytheas and Medea stopped next to Cadmus and Hipponax just inside the open door; Aria advanced next to Hippocrates to look at Orion, still unconscious in his bed. She had heard the rumors about the terrible crash that were circulating through the crowds in many different versions, some closer to the truth than others, the one element in common that Orion already had died. Now relieved, despite Orion's dire condition, that the stories were not true, tears streamed down her cheeks.

"Stand back please," instructed the physician, issuing Aria a kindly but firm nod. "Let me do my work."

"Come," whispered Cadmus, gently leading Aria back to join the position behind the physician from where all who loved Orion watched in silence as Hippocrates began treatment. First the doctor placed a compress of healing herbs over the large knot above his patient's forehead. Next he stemmed the bleeding from the array of shallow cuts and scrapes distributed over Orion's face and body, after which he cleaned and bandaged each. Then he turned his attention to the assortment of bumps and bruises covering the young man's body, placing more compresses of healing herbs over these.

"Now we must wait," Hippocrates solemnly informed everyone. "There is nothing more I can do for your friend."

Aria walked over to the bed, sat down, and held Orion's hand. She did not let it go for one second during the four hours that Orion slept, breathing shallow and labored as he fought against going over the precipice into forever.

Suddenly, Orion coughed and stirred, and his breathing became stronger. Hippocrates, who had moved to a chair away from his patient while he waited, now rose and walked forward, hopeful. Aria got up from the bed and receded out of his way to stand with the others near the door.

Slowly, Orion opened his eyes, blinking as he tried to focus his blurry vision.

"How do you feel?" Hippocrates asked.

"My head hurts," Orion replied, confused by the fog of a con-cussion. "What happened?"

"You had an accident," explained Hippocrates. "We were wor-ried that you would not make it."

"Did I win?" Orion asked, curiously optimistic. "The last thing I remember was heading for the tunnel in the lead."

"Well, not exactly," Hipponax said, stumbling to find the right way to explain the crash. He wanted to distress Orion as little as possible.

"How does that feel?" asked Hippocrates, removing the com-press to knead his fingers against the deep-purple and black bruise over the left side of Orion's rib cage. Orion grimaced. Even the experienced physician's touch caused intense pain.

"You cracked some ribs on this side," the doctor observed as he replaced the compress. Then he turned to Hipponax and Cadmus. "I need you to sit him up."

Cadmus and Hipponax, supporting behind, helped grimacing Orion up to sitting, and Hippocrates wound a white bandage around the injury. When done, the doctor retreated to the chair, opened his black leather pouch, took out three small packets wrapped with white gauze, and handed them to Aria. "Here are some herbs. Make a tea, and give him a full cup every three hours. I'll come back to check on him in the morning. With a lot of rest and excellent care, in time he should make a full recovery."

Then the doctor left for the night, mindful of his other patients scattered throughout Olympia. But he did not go before receiving the profuse gratitude due to him, especially when he refused payment saying that his enjoyment of Orion's performance at the games had been reward enough already.

❧

When the games were first announced, word of them reached even the Helots. But their Spartan masters forbade the Helots from attending the event under threat of death. And there was no reason for any among the slaves to doubt that would be the punishment for disobeying the mandate. Centuries ago, the Helots had fought a bitter hundred-year war, trying to stave off subjugation. And even now the bravest of their number rumbled with the cry of freedom. Yet the overlords, through a series of terror measures, were able to maintain their dominance. The Spartans formed a secret society of soldiers (the Krypteia) that would come by night to kill, in savage fashion, any Helot who stood out from among his peers for excellence—be it in strength, ingenuity, or defiance. Once, when Sparta had fought Argos long ago, the Spartans gathered the strongest Helot males and promised them freedom in exchange for service against the Argives. Then the masters executed all those who stepped forward to accept the offer, considering them too brave to live.

Despite the fact that the Spartans could be expected to make good on their threat, one Helot, Nestor, who resembled Orion in all but the jet-black color of his hair, attended anyway. The twenty-one-year-old from the village of Messenia never had any stomach for injustice, and he came in search of learning something or meeting someone who could help him bestow liberty on his own people.

Since arriving at Olympia, Nestor had tried to stay out of sight of the Spartan soldiers, some of whom, back at home, already suspected he was a fitting candidate for a nighttime visit from the Krypteia. Yet, in the last two days, Nestor had wandered Olympia more boldly; his growing hunger to know more about people from other places, fed by all he had seen and heard, had gotten the better of his limited capacity for caution in the face of oppression.

And now, at eleven, on the night after the chariot race, Nestor roamed the grounds of the Old Stadium, constantly whipping his head in every direction to drink in the lively activity all around him. Performers of all kinds regaled the crowds, composed of people from each of the attending locales except the Amazon island and Sparta. And now the people of the six cities mingled freely with one another. Groups of spectators—many composed of varying nationalities—laughed and ate together. And their conversations, in addition to the games, turned to other things, including the war between Athens and Sparta.

But as enthralled as Nestor was, determined to fulfill the purpose for which he had risked everything to come to Olympia, he approached a group of several men; they were standing around laughing uncontrollably at a story told by the one among them who seemed to suck all attention in his direction.

Sixty-year-old Herodotus (short, slender, and bald) was originally from Halicarnassus, a city populated by people of Greek origins but located in Asia Minor and ruled by a puppet Greek tyrant on behalf of Persian overlords. At twenty-five, the son of a prominent merchant fled the place of his birth when he was implicated in a failed coup against these masters. He spent the next thirty-five years traveling through Asia Minor, Egypt, and Greece. Having recorded the histories of the places he visited, now he came to Olympia to tell his stories and to chronicle the current events as they happened. After all, he was the only writer who conducted a systematic inquiry into happenings to discover cause and effect. His critics, however, jealously maintained that he often resorted to fairytale explanations to render the facts more fantastic and called him the Father of Fabrication rather than the Father of History, by which title he should rightfully be known.

"Excuse me, sir," Nestor said, tapping Herodotus on the shoulder from behind. The Father of History, dressed like a resident of Athens, his current home, seemed like the kind of man who would have an answer to the Helot's questions.

"Yes," said Herodotus, turning around. He was pleased that Nestor, clearly recognizing his prominence, had chosen him from among the whole group; the rest of the group now stood by watching.

"I seek an audience with one of the ambassadors from Athens," said Nestor. "Can you direct me to him?"

Nestor had made a rather unusual request that clearly carried a heavy agenda. It warranted a more private conversation. "And what may I ask is your purpose?" inquired Herodotus, taking Nestor by the arm and leading him away from the group, which resumed conversation behind.

Then, both of them risking that the other was a Spartan spy, Nestor confided his reasons to Herodotus. Fully convinced, the Father of History agreed to lead the Helot to Cleon in the Ambassador Quarters. Herodotus was a renowned writer, and the Spartans sought a favorable accounting from him. They would allow him into where the dignitaries were housed, and he could, with the Helot changing clothes, pass Nestor off as his scribe.

Within half an hour, Herodotus and Nestor found themselves sitting with Cleon on three cushioned, high-back chairs in the Athenian Speaker's lavish room. Cleon, rather than looking down on Nestor, treated him like an honored guest. The slave was astounded that such an important man received him at all—let alone so warmly.

"So how may I help you?" inquired Cleon; he held out an earthen bowl to offer Nestor some deep-purple grapes.

"No, thank you," replied Nestor, politely refusing the fruit. Though he had not eaten well, he hungered more for knowledge. "I'm not sure where to start."

"The beginning always works for me," said Cleon, smiling as he tried humor to put his tense visitor at ease. Clearly, the young man was somewhat overwhelmed.

Nestor paused. Then he spoke. "I have heard a lot of things about your way of life. I am curious how it all works. It has to be better than the Spartan way."

"Go on," replied Cleon, intending to make the visitor speak to make certain of his true purpose. Despite Herodotus vouching for the Helot, the Athenian Speaker now wondered about Nestor's motivation for bringing such a highly charged subject so readily to the fore.

"Long ago, the Spartans invaded the surrounding villages and made us their slaves," Nestor continued, not sure what to say, yet eager to spill his frustration to a willing ear. "Now they force us to grow food for them and then deny us a fair share of what we make. Many go without, while our masters have more than they need."

"That must be difficult to endure," replied Cleon, instantly convinced of his visitor's sincerity. Nestor's passion burned too deep to be anything other than real, and his manner was too humble to be Spartan bred.

"It is," replied Nestor, more serious. "But we also hunger for more than food. We hunger for our basic rights to think and speak for ourselves."

"Even this is denied you?" asked Cleon, more out of encouraging Nestor to vent his troubles rather than out of a need to hear facts he already understood as true. All Greeks were meant to be free. The Spartans' enslavement of their neighbors was a well-known subject of discontent to those from other cities, especially Cleon. He had been instrumental in giving the people of his home more liberties than enjoyed by anyone outside Athens.

"Yes, this most of all," explained Nestor. "The Spartans fear new ideas more than anything else and punish those who speak them with very painful deaths, especially those who talk of your ways."

"The Athenian way is indeed different," Cleon agreed, feeding his visitor's starvation. "Our system is built on freedoms. We elect our leaders, and they represent the people by openly receiving and considering all new ideas, even from strangers to our city."

"I have heard that your ways have brought great prosperity," asked Nestor, curiously. "Is that so?"

"It is," proudly explained Cleon. "When allowed to live in peace, Athens thrives in every way, even as a center for the arts and literature."

Herodotus smiled, having taken the last of Cleon's statement as a compliment directed at him personally.

Nestor was now dreamy-eyed at the prospect of such a society. "I would give anything to have my people live like you do."

"To achieve this," Cleon instructed, "you must inspire them. For such things can spring forth only from the people themselves."

"That won't be easy," noted Nestor, shaking his head.

"It seldom is," replied Cleon. "But it can be done if you plan carefully how to reach your goal."

"We outnumber the Spartans ten to one, and though we want to change things, not enough of us believe that we can, so we don't act," Nestor said, explaining what he regarded as the primary obstacle, mindful of how fearful most Helots were of their masters.

"And how do you suppose that might change?" asked Cleon, intentionally turning the discussion away from focusing on the problem to a search for the solution.

"What my people need is a symbol," Nestor replied, quickly learning the lesson of where to apply his mental energies. "They need something to show them that all things are possible."

Chapter Fourteen

A POINTED END

When Orion stirred the next morning, he found Aria sitting at the side of his cot holding his hand. She had spent the whole night there, watching while he rested and waking him every few hours to administer the prescribed medicine. Everyone else, though now awake, had fallen asleep at different points during the vigil, mindful that Aria alone held the best hope of soothing Orion's pain.

"How do you feel?" she asked.

"My ribs are sore," Orion replied, with a surprised expression, as Aria helped him up to sitting. "Other than that, I feel much better than expected. Even my head seems better. What time is it, Cadmus?"

"Time for more rest," replied Cadmus, now standing behind Aria, suspicious. "What are you doing up so early?"

"I have to get to the stadium," Orion said as Aria helped him out of his cot to standing.

"Get back in bed," Hipponax said, chiming in with his own concern. "You don't need to watch the javelin competition. You need to rest."

"What do you mean *watch?*" replied Orion, assertively plucking his three javelins from where he had placed them at the beginning of the games, standing upright in the far corner of his room. There the eight-foot-long wooden shafts, shaved to a point at their tips, had remained untouched, waiting for this moment.

"You can't be serious," Hipponax protested, just as Hippocrates, returning to check on his patient, walked in. "Doctor, he wants to compete."

"Young man, you are too injured," warned Hippocrates. "You could cause permanent damage to your body. A disabled life is not an easy one."

"Did you hear that, Orion?" Cadmus asked emphatically. "Now get back in bed."

Orion held fast, more determined than before, refusing to retreat to the cot. He had come too far and overcome too much to turn back now, even if that meant he would be carried sprawled from the arena floor. It was a small price to pay for knowing that he had given his absolute best when called by fate.

"Maybe you can talk some sense into him," Cadmus appealed to Aria, expecting that she, too, would urge Orion not to compete.

"It is his decision," Aria replied, putting her hand on Orion's shoulder in an unyielding show of support. She knew what Orion wanted. She would never stand in the way of his dreams, even with such high stakes in play.

❧

Soon after, Orion stood with his three shafts at the center of the arena floor. The bandages were gone from around his midsection; remarkably, the bruising over his ribs was gone too. The infusions prescribed by Hippocrates indeed had worked miracles.

Demosthenes, Archidamus, Memnon, and Penthesilea stood next to Orion, each ready for the start of the final day of competition, javelins in hand. Herak and Konon were too injured to participate due to their crash in the chariot race. And Argive had died when his cart overturned in the stadium as he rushed towards the tunnel at the start of the contest.

In the terraces, the buzzing stadium crowd now sat mostly intermingled—no longer divided by nationality but by character; those of similar natures had found their own kind from among the people from various other places. However, the band of fierce female warriors—grouped together above the stadium exit—still refused company other than their own sisters.

Cadmus and Hipponax accompanied Aria, Medea, and Pytheas in the front terrace row, almost directly behind the ambassador chairs on the left of the bowl. As usual, Lycurgus sat in the middle of the Hellanodikes in his ornate chair on the opposite side. And his men, in full battle ensemble, ringed the arena grass.

The trumpeters, standing on both sides of the row of ambassadors, sounded a blast, and the crowd fell silent as Ibycus walked out from among the soldiers to join the athletes at center-stage.

"After two exciting days of competition, we have but five athletes left standing before us," Ibycus announced, "and I can hear exactly what you are thinking. Which one of these magnificent specimens will rise to win the games, thereby writing his name into history?"

The terraces, much to his delight, readily agreed.

"Then, without further delay," the flamboyant showman continued, "it is my pleasure to present the final preliminary event. Many regard it as the ultimate test of athleticism. Combining strength with accuracy, I give you the javelin!"

The entire terrace crowd (even Amazons) applauded as Ibycus returned to the side of the arena floor. Meanwhile, the athletes, shafts in hand, walked towards the far end of the grass oval.

Then, in anticipation of the start, the applause stopped as the competitors arrived at the seven-foot-tall, sturdy wooden stake where the garland of olive leaves had rested during the chariot race. Still planted firmly in the ground, thirty yards from the Spartans at the end of the grass, no champion's crest topped it today. Instead, an identical wooden pole had been planted across the length of the arena floor, twenty yards directly in front of the stadium tunnel. Also devoid of any crown, it was the target at which the athletes would cast their missiles from behind the stake where they now stood.

Suddenly, five Spartans entered the stadium through the tunnel. They were followed by five more, dragging Helot Nestor along behind by the long tail of the rough, brown rope tied around his waist and hands. A separate piece of coarse cord wrapped tightly around his head and through his open mouth to prevent him from issuing more than a muffled grunt. A Spartan patrol had recognized Nestor the night before, while he roamed Olympia alone, after having parted with Cleon and Herodotus. Immediately, they took him into custody for breaking the ban on Helots attending the games. But even as they did, knowing that his own life was done, Nestor spoke defiantly of his people one day casting off the Spartan yoke and forever putting an end to their way of life.

Now the five Spartans at the fore marched towards the closer wooden pole, passed, and then stopped some ten yards in front of it, standing side-by-side, facing the athletes at the far end of the stadium. Meanwhile, the other five Spartans hauled Nestor to the target stake and began fastening him to it with the long tail of the rope by which they had led him. First, they bound his waist to the pole. Next, they wound the cord down around his legs. Last, they coiled the rope back up the entire length of his body to his neck and wrapped it tightly around the pole, almost choking him.

Clearly, Nestor was the intended mark, a fact that did not seem to bother either Penthesilea or Memnon. But Orion and Demosthenes were horrified—exactly the reaction the two kings intended by introducing a human target. Orion and Demosthenes, the two event winners (either of whom could become Olympic Grand Champion by winning the last preliminary event) would, motivated by compassion, surely balk at piercing such a goal, thereby giving Archidamus a better chance to prevail. Now Archidamus smirked at

the disgust written on their faces, and then he exchanged a satisfied glance with Lycurgus, who nodded back approvingly.

Orion and Demosthenes looked at one another and nodded.
Then, without a word, both stabbed two javelins into the ground,
and together, each holding a single spear, they began walking down
towards the stake at the tunnel end.

A hundred Spartans, from all sides, converged to engulf Demosthenes and Orion before they traveled half the distance. Now the
two champions were surrounded by row upon row of pointed
spears and shining bronze shields with blood-red Spartan insignia
blazed across their faces.

"Let us through," commanded Demosthenes.

"I don't think so," barked the same Spartan captain who two
nights previous had abducted the athletes from their rooms to
deliver them to the Temple of Zeus.

The Olympic Games always had honored Zeus through noble
competition. From the beginning, when the Spartans came to Olympia with armed men, they had lost face with the people from the
other Greek cities, even those who were their allies in the war
outside. It seemed to everyone that by flouting the competition's
proper purposes, the Spartans were blatantly insulting both them
and the highest of all gods at the same time. And as the events
progressed, each additional Spartan corruption had increasingly
irked the people from the other Greek cities and had turned them
further against the self-proclaimed hosts. Now, with Nestor on the
stake, the terrace crowd (except the Amazons) was fully disgusted
that the Spartans, even more than before, were defiling the sacred

spirit of the Olympic Games. And the spectators stirred deeply dissatisfied, some even calling insults to the Spartan kings.

The ring of Spartans standing at the edge of the arena floor facing arena-center—where a hundred of their comrades surrounded Demosthenes and Orion—now turned threateningly to face the terraces.

The crowd quieted.

"This is barbaric," Cleon, rising from his seat in the ambassadors' row of ornate chairs, shouted to Lycurgus, seated across the way. "What has the man tied to the stake done to deserve this?" The Spartans would clearly use force against the spectators to impose their agenda, a course that Cleon was determined to avoid at all costs. Yet, Cleon could not let an innocent man go to his death unaided.

"He is one of our Helots," replied Lycurgus, voice resonating strong and determined through the whole quiet bowl. "And he has violated our order to stay away from the games."

"Surely, this is not the punishment for such a questionable offense," protested Cleon. "Besides, the Olympic Games are not the place for this."

"He is guilty of sedition, a crime in Sparta punishable by death," insisted Lycurgus. "The event will proceed as planned. But you are free to withdraw your representative if you want." The rules required an athlete to compete in every preliminary event. Stepping down from this competition would immediately eliminate Demosthenes from becoming Olympic Grand Champion.

"Give me a moment to consult with our athlete," answered Cleon, motioning to Demosthenes to come over to him. Now, with force threatened against the spectators, he and Demosthenes would have to choose between what options Lycurgus allowed them.

"As you wish," replied Lycurgus, smug that he had regained control.

Demosthenes pushed his way through the reluctantly parting rows of spears and shields around him and Orion. Then he walked towards Cleon, standing a few feet in front of the ten ambassador chairs. Meanwhile, Orion, encircled again (the spears and shields closed quickly behind Demosthenes to keep the Elean contained), turned defiantly to Lycurgus and raised his own protest in the hope that it would change things. "Give him his last words. It is his right!"

"Last words!" the terrace crowd (except Amazons) chanted, defying the Spartan intimidation to defend the most basic of rights, given all condemned men throughout Greece and considered by every civilized person as fundamental to the human dignity of both executed and executioner. "Last words! Last words!"

Lycurgus signaled with his hands for quiet. Then he spoke. "I am pleased you brought that up. He already had his last words. He wants you all to know that he is truly sorry for his wayward actions and that he fully accepts his punishment as a tribute to his kings. However, that being said, his kings are also merciful. If he makes it through unscathed, we will let him go free."

Now Nestor's eyes flashed wild with protest at the lies.

"The athlete from Athens will compete," Cleon agreed, and Demosthenes walked over to rejoin the others standing next to the pole from which they would throw.

"What about you, sheepherder?" Lycurgus asked Orion. "Do you withdraw?"

Orion stayed silent for a moment, considering his alternatives before he spoke. He, like the others, was powerless to prevent the event from proceeding in the manner forced by the Spartans under threat of greater harm against the spectators. By withdrawing, he would accomplish nothing except make it easier for Archidamus to win. And the Spartan king, of all people, clearly did not deserve the honor of becoming Olympic Grand Champion. Besides, Nestor stood a reasonable chance of surviving the contest and regaining his freedom. "I will continue but under protest. This defies the spirit of the games."

"Then let it begin," shouted Lycurgus. "We've wasted enough time."

In the middle of the arena, the hundred Spartans reluctantly backed away from Orion, allowing the young Elean to walk free as they joined their comrades at the edge of the competition floor.

"I'll go first," Penthesilea scowled at her adversaries as Orion arrived at the other athletes. "Get out of my way!"

As the rest of the competitors moved to the left side of the stake at the throwing end, Penthesilea, her three pointed missiles in hand, walked eighty-seven feet back, towards the Spartans direct-ly in front of the grass oval's end. There, a yard in front of them, she stabbed two of her javelins into the ground. Each slender five-foot-long shaft (painted with the spots of a jaguar and tipped with razor-sharp bronze) stood upright and proud. When word of the games had first reached Penthesilea, she scoured her jungle-island home for the perfect wood to craft, over many hours of delicate work, into equipment that resembled the spears used by the Amazons in war.

Now the stadium was dead silent, waiting, as she turned to face the terrified human target tied to the stake at the opposite end of the arena floor, twenty yards from the exit tunnel.

"Eeeeeeehhhh," Penthesilea, breaking into a run, screamed loud and shrill, javelin pointed skyward in her trailing right hand. Then she reached to the right of the throwing pole and launched her missile, putting the entire weight of her body into the wild cast.

The javelin sliced up through the air, zipping towards Nestor across the length of the arena. And as it approached, he desperately tried, to no avail, to free himself from the ropes that bound him tight to the target stake. Then, as the missile neared, he tensed to receive it. But to his relief, the javelin flew over his head, wide left; then it continued on to strike hard against the side of the stadium tunnel's arch, breaking the wooden shaft in two, a foot from its bronze tip.

Penthesilea, snarling all the while, returned to her starting position, grabbed her second sleek leopard shaft from the ground, let out another shrill scream as she broke into a run, reached the throwing pole, and again launched wildly.

This bronze-tipped death stick, like its predecessor, sliced up through the air, zipping towards Nestor across the length of the arena. This time, having accepted its futility, he did not try to free himself; instead, he simply awaited the shaft's arrival, every muscle engaged in anticipation of the impact. But again, the javelin flew

over his head, even higher, this time wide right; then it, too, continued on to strike the archway over the stadium tunnel (this time
at the top), and then it bounced straight back to land on the
ground, miraculously not shattered.

Penthesilea, fully enraged by her own inability to throw with
precision (the Amazons in war rained their spears with volume
over accuracy) stormed back, more determined than before, to her
last Amazon spear, standing proud in the ground, a symbol of her
entire sisterhood. She grabbed it. Then, piercing the air with her
scream, she ran at the mark, let fly, and the javelin sliced towards
the scared target at the tunnel end.

But this third toss was even wilder than the first two, Penthesilea having failed to control her muscles, made taut by anger.
Sailing high and to the left, her javelin headed directly towards the
section of the stadium terraces above the tunnel that was occupied
exclusively by her sisters. Now the Amazons frantically scattered
away from where they thought it would land, as the wood, carefully
culled from their own island home and fashioned in their image,
sliced towards them.

The javelin came down in the center of where the Amazons had
parted a circle. But its bronze point glanced hard on the stone at
the back of the step on which it landed. And then the spear, razor tip
first, began skating along the width of the same step—towards the
feet of those to the left of the gap—forcing them to jump and scam-
per with animal agility to barely avoid it piercing their naked feet.

Minutes later, Demosthenes stood ready to make his final throw; his first two javelins were already planted upright in the ground within an inch of each other, three feet in front of Nestor. The eight-foot-long wooden shafts (each shaved to a point at the tip, then painted white except for the blue band around the center of its medium girth) had been carefully crafted to accommodate the specific needs of the sport rather than to match weapons of war. These were perfectly weighted (not too light or sturdy) and balanced instruments (slightly heavier at the leading end). In the proper hands, they could glide and land with absolute precision.

Demosthenes ran at the pole, reached, and then threw, effortless and smooth. His torpedo glided gracefully through the air, right at Nestor. But then, like the two before it, the javelin dipped slightly and then dropped, planting in the grass within an inch of its brothers.

Now the terraces, except the hissing Amazons, applauded long and strong as Demosthenes raised his hands over his head, proudly receiving their praise. The Athenian general, renowned for his skill in this sport, easily could have struck the mark, yet he chose not to. Instead, he had planted his three rods like a curtain (albeit a narrow one) in front of the center of the target to deflect the incoming spears of those who followed. At the same time, Demosthenes had given himself the opportunity to win, by coming as close to Nestor as possible without the risk of hitting him. If no other competitor could land more proximate to the target, then he would become champion of the javelin toss and the games.

❧

Now it was Memnon's turn, and the ambassadors from Mantinea called him over to their chairs to instruct him not to aim at Nestor but to land his shafts as Demosthenes had just done. The African warrior-for-hire agreed to comply with their wishes. But he had no intention of doing so. And he returned to his three javelins, already planted in the grass a yard in front of the ring of Spartans, ready to pierce the target with the first of his four-foot-long spears. Heavy, thick, stone-tipped, dark-wood weapons (each adorned with a zebra-skin grip) that resembled those he had used as a boy to hunt the striped animal at the waterholes in his native continent. Meant primarily for throwing at close range or in hand-to-hand combat, such shafts since then had seen him through many perilous adventures, and now he found no reason to abandon his trusted tools in favor of another design, with which he did not have years of practice. He would rise or fall with what he knew.

Memnon grabbed one up. Then, shaft in hand, he ran at the pole, reached, and launched. His spear arced up high into the air over the arena floor, higher than the top of the stadium, forcing even those seated around the upper rim of the bowl to look up to fathom its fight.

Still rising, it crossed the halfway point, and then it slowed and dipped, again picking up speed as it descended towards the target.

Nestor tensed as he watched it honing in. Then he closed his eyes as the spear landed inches above his head with the thud of stone against wood. There it remained, stuck in the flat top of the stake.

Drops of nervous sweat trickled down Nestor's head onto his face. The cold Ethiopian hunter, who had returned to the starting position at the far end of the grass oval to begin his second cycle, posed a greater threat than anyone else so far.

Again Memnon ran at the start, reached the pole, and launched. The second spear, in identical fashion to the prior, arced up high over the arena floor and continued to rise until it crossed the halfway point. Then it slowed, dipped, and sped up again as it descended towards the target.

Nestor, more scared than before, tightened every muscle as he watched it coming, and then he closed his eyes as the stone tip, having avoided the three javelins placed by Demosthenes, planted hard in the ground, throwing up a clump of grassy soil, inches in front of his feet.

A torrent of sweat streamed down Nestor's head and face as, anticipating the worst, he watched Memnon return to his starting position and clutch up the remaining spear by its zebra grip.

The entire stadium crowd, also expecting a bad end, held its breath as the Ethiopian ran forward and threw. Now that the hunter had gauged the target with the others of its kind, by this last shaft, he would surely make his kill.

The spear soared to its apex, plummeted, and then thudded into the stake—exactly in the four-inch space between Nestor's knees, leaving him miraculously unscathed. The crowd (not the Amazons though) vented its collective relief with sighs that matched the one issued by the tormented captive.

A minute later, Orion stood at the throwing stake with a javelin in his right hand and the other two stuck upright in the ground next to him. The eight-foot-long wooden shafts (which in architecture looked remarkably like Demosthenes' perfectly balanced Athenian-crafted instruments) were painted only with three two-inch-wide green bands, equally spaced by that same distance around the middle. Cadmus himself had made Orion's equipment from wood cut out of the trunk of a stately old mountain pine that still graced a hillside near their farm. And though pinewood was not the material used by anyone else to construct shafts, Orion's javelins, like him, now occupied the grandest of stages, unassuming yet confident representatives of their simple and good way of life.

Orion (body still facing towards the target at the other end) turned his head towards Lycurgus, sitting halfway down on the left. Now the young Champion of Elis locked eyes with the powerful king. Without breaking his stare, Orion defiantly hurled his first javelin hard into the ground in front of himself, a yard beyond the throwing pole. Never breaking his gaze, he plucked the second shaft from its place, did the same, and then repeated, in exact manner, with the third.

The terrace crowd as one (save the section of she-leopards) surged to its feet with thunderous applause for Orion's bold refusal to play the Spartans' game. The crowd had wondered, somewhat hopefully, what the Elean, ambassador of the spirit of the Olympics, would do when he first stepped to the line, pointed pine pole in

hand. Now that he had surpassed even the spectators' most exact-
ing hopes, they were deeply satisfied that the sacred ideal of noble
competition, flagging in all other competitors except Demosthenes,
still rode elevated on his shoulders.

"Stupid sheepherder," Archidamus scowled at Orion, instantly
pulling the Elean's attention away from Lycurgus. "You think you
can save him? Watch this."

Archidamus plucked one of his javelins from the ground to the
left of the throwing pole. Though similar in length and girth to
those of Demosthenes and Orion, his instruments, heavier and
more deadly pointed, were made of solid bronze, polished to maximum luster.

Now the entire crowd silenced as Archidamus walked up to the
right of the throwing pole and looked directly at trembling Nestor.
Then, without any run up, Archidamus yelped as he heaved his
missile forward with incredible brute force. "Yaaaaaah!"

The solid bronze rod zipped flat, cutting through the arena air,
straight, with no arc, right at its target, homing in as if guided by
some unseen force.

Nestor watched as the javelin approached for a sure hit, filling
him with the terror of impending death just before it broke
through the curtain of shafts placed by Demosthenes. Then it
pierced clean through the middle of Nestor's chest and planted,
with a thud, in the stake behind. For a surreal second, Nestor,
shocked, looked at the javelin sticking through him. Then his life
went out, and he dropped limp, eyes still open wide in disbelief.

Except for the stirring Amazons, the terrace crowd sat in

complete silence, disgusted. Once more, the cynical Spartans had slapped the spectators and Zeus in the face. And this time the Spartans were also spitting on both them and God too.

Lycurgus was more than a little pleased that Archidamus had prevailed by landing his javelin in the meat of the target. And now the older king smiled sarcastically as he leaned over and commented to Solorchus, the Chief Hellanodike, sitting to his right. "It looks like we have a winner."

"Aaeee!" Antiope, the scar-faced Amazon queen, screeched as she rose from her seat, suddenly and violently shattering the relative quiet in the stadium with her ear-piercing cry. Then, flapping her arms like a bird readying for flight, she jumped down to the grass from the terraces above the tunnel. The closest Spartans, at first startled, pointing their spears and readying their shields, now turned to face the threat. But she did not advance on them. Instead, squawking and waving her wings, Antiope turned and stormed into the tunnel. And the rest of her pride streamed over the terraces to follow, hissing at the nearby Spartan vigil. The soldiers of the blood-red and shining bronze just stood their ground and let the Amazons pass. The she-leopards were clearly leaving and posed no danger—a fact confirmed when Penthesilea ran off the arena floor to join her sisters.

"Such poor sports," Lycurgus commented sarcastically to Solorchus. "You think they would at least stay to watch the final event."

But the Amazons had no such intention ever since their representative—having failed to land one shaft even close to the target—had been eliminated (from the javelin toss and from the games) by the first competitor, Demosthenes, who did. And the feral females had remained in the stadium, after that moment, only in the hope of witnessing the sort of end to the javelin that Archidamus provided.

Chapter Fifteen

PANKRATION

The Spartans removed Nestor's dead shell from the stake and carted it from the stage. Minutes later, Orion, Demosthenes, and Archidamus stood at arena center. Next to them, Ibycus, flamboyant as ever in his blue tunic, addressed the crowd (still shocked but surging with anticipation). "This is the moment we have all been awaiting—the final event to decide which athlete will be crowned Olympic Grand Champion. And so, according to the rules of these games, we now turn to the hosts to tell us what that final event will be. What say you, gracious Lycurgus?"

The final event was usually decided by all the attending cities together. Yet here, Sparta had insisted that it, as host, be allowed the sole prerogative of choosing the final event, which everyone now waited for Lycurgus to exercise. Surely, the Spartan king would select the sport with the most storied history and tradition of honor at the Olympic Games: the footrace in armor down the full length of the arena.

Lycurgus took his time, enjoying making everyone wait, and then he shouted "pankration," and the terraces jolted to life, buzzing with a combination of shock and excitement.

Orion, never having heard of such a sport, was confused. In the crowd, Aria, echoing her hero's thoughts, turned curiously to her father; she was wearing a worried expression. "What is pankration?"

"It is a Spartan fighting sport," he explained.

"Everything is allowed except gouging the eyes or biting, but there is no referee to enforce that anyway. The winner is the last man standing. The losers often die."

Aria's face turned ice-cold, as did those of Cadmus, Hipponax, and Medea. All four were staggered, none of them ever having heard of such a barbaric event.

Meanwhile, at arena-center, the athletes each drew one of the three straws that Ibycus offered in his right hand, length obscured. Then Orion, Demosthenes, and Archidamus each held up his own to compare. The Elean had pulled the longest, a full two inches more than the matching three inches proffered by the other two competitors.

"Archidamus and Demosthenes first," announced Ibycus. "Orion fights the winner."

Orion and Ibycus moved off to stand among the ring of Spartan troops at the sides of the arena floor—Ibycus to the right, near the seated jackals, and Orion to the left, near his friends.

Archidamus and Demosthenes immediately began circling each
other. The Athenian general had never participated in the pankration, and he was somewhat unfamiliar with what types of mechan-
ics to expect from its most renowned practitioner, whom he now
faced.

"You have no idea how long I've waited for this," taunted Archidamus. "I'm going to tear you apart, piece by piece."

"You seem to have forgotten," Demosthenes replied, "the last
time we met, you were hiding behind two of your men."

Archidamus motioned as if he were about to unleash a punch,
but he did not let it go. Demosthenes overreacted to the feint,
blinking his eyes and blocking in anticipation of a blow that never
came.

"Nervous, are we?" smirked the Spartan king. Suddenly, he
stormed in with a brutal attack—kicking, punching, and hitting
with everything driving Demosthenes to the ground.

Archidamus continued the savage onslaught on the fallen
Demosthenes until the Athenian general grabbed his enemy's foot
and twisted his ankle to topple him away.

Both men rose, Demosthenes holding his face and Archidamus
gingerly stepping on his twisted ankle, and once more they circled
each other, ready to pounce.

Archidamus pretended another lunge. Again Demosthenes,
clearly out of his element and unsure how to interpret his adversary's movements, overreacted.

This drew a smile from the Spartan right before he rushed in
again without warning.

Now, however, Demosthenes was better able to gauge the coming storm, and he kept his feet. For a while, the two battled back and forth evenly—a violent exchange of blows of all kinds—until Archidamus caught Demosthenes with a devastating series of four unanswered punches to the head.

Stunned, Demosthenes stood in front of Archidamus, too weak and groggy to resist as the massive Spartan brute, one hand around the general's neck and the other around his left knee, lifted him up off his feet. As if he were pressing a barbell, Archidamus swept Demosthenes skyward until he was holding the Athenian general high above his head—keeping him there for a moment and then slamming him down hard into the ground. Demosthenes, landing on his back, hit the arena grass with a thud. And there he lay motionless, barely conscious.

Archidamus went to one knee over Demosthenes. With his left hand, the king grabbed the general by the hair and lifted his head slightly off the ground. Demosthenes gazed up at Archidamus, helpless, as the Spartan king raised his right hand, readying to deliver a finishing blow. Now Archidamus, breaking the stare, looked up at Lycurgus, who responded with a nod, indicating his approval.

Aria, horrified, turned to Pytheas. "Why doesn't anyone stop it?"

"Demosthenes chose to fight of his own free will," her father replied solemnly. "Now he must face what has been dealt him as a man."

Archidamus looked down again, right into Demosthenes' eyes, which knew the end was near. But just as Archidamus was about to strike, a pair of feet appeared—standing in front of him—on the other side of the prone Athenian general.

Startled, the Spartan king looked up to find Orion. No Spartan at arena-side had seen the young hero approaching, and thus no one had warned Archidamus. Lycurgus had been busy gloating to the Hellanodikes, and his soldiers were all facing the crowd to intimidate.

Orion, not wasting the element of surprise, kicked Archidamus in the chest, sprawling him back and away. Then the Elean stepped over Demosthenes, placing himself between the fallen Athenian general and his stunned adversary. This was a new Orion, more determined than ever and without fear, unwilling to stand back any longer and allow others to suffer cruelty without making a full stand for them, regardless of any other considerations.

"I know you Helots like to suffer, but can't you wait your turn?" taunted Archidamus, rising slowly while he assessed the situation, determined to deal the man he now equated with a slave in the same fashion as he had destroyed Demosthenes. Orion, like Demosthenes, had never participated in pankration. And perhaps Orion would be even easier to defeat. He had far less experience in other forms of combat than the Athenian general, whom Archidamus had just easily left splayed on the floor.

Archidamus, having regained his feet, smiled as he and Orion began circling each other. Behind them, Cleon and three other ambassadors carted Demosthenes off to their side.

Archidamus, still smiling, feinted. But to his surprise, Orion did not react and instead calmly motioned him to move forward. "Come on."

The king, angered by what he regarded as the sheepherder's arrogance, attacked. Orion, combining lightning reflexes with his innate sense of balance, easily sidestepped his assailant's charge and swept his forearm across Archidamus' neck, putting the brute down hard.

"Ooh!" reacted the entire terrace crowd.

Still down and smarting from the blow, Archidamus held his throat. As he waited for the Spartan to get up, Orion—his growing contempt for the king boiling to the surface—did some taunting of his own. "That was for Demosthenes."

Archidamus came to his feet, realizing the Elean would not be easy to beat; and now the king moved more cautiously as he and Orion began circling each other again.

"Come on," Orion taunted again.

The anger flooding his veins destroying all discretion, Archidamus lunged again, and again Orion sidestepped him, this time taking the Spartan king down with a leg sweep.

"That was for the man on the stake," shouted Orion, with growing confidence that he would teach the Spartan a bitter lesson on the competition floor. "Get up!"

Archidamus, furious but now determined not to allow his anger again to distract him from his usual focus, rose and cautiously moved towards Orion. Suddenly, when close enough, he launched a fierce attack of punches and kicks, much like the offensive with which he had demolished Demosthenes.

At first, Orion, proving more resilient than his predecessor, evaded and blocked most of the assault, landing his own powerful counters. He was clearly getting the better of the fight until one of Archidamus' punches struck him in the previously injured ribs, cracking them further and sending a shock wave of pain through his whole body. Now Orion, grimacing noticeably, backed away, his expression changing from total confidence to desperate worry.

"What have we here?" taunted the Spartan, the cynical smile returning to his face, this time more sinister, as he launched another furious assault, clearly designed to exploit the newly discovered weak spot.

At first, Orion was still strong enough to effectively counter and evade, and the massive brute had difficulty finding his ribs with any frequency. But as the onslaught progressed, each successive blow that Archidamus landed to Orion's cage, bruising purple again, increasingly hurt and weakened the Elean. With every passing second, Archidamus become more able to find his prime target as Orion became less able to dodge and less able to land his own shots. Soon, battered Orion was reduced to a purely defensive combatant, and he was absorbing terrible punishment.

Archidamus moved in for the kill, putting the noble Elean down with a knee to the midsection that left him rolling on the ground, holding his ribs in agony and coughing up blood. Now the Spartan king, fully confident the fight was won, with his arms raised in victory, strutted like a proud peacock as he demeaned his beaten foe by reminding Orion of the moment when he had been afraid to get up against Memnon in the boxing final. "What's the matter, Helot? Lost your nerve again?"

At arena-side, Lycurgus delighted in Spartan prowess. In the terraces, the silent spectators were depressed at the sight of their destroyed hero; it was as if all of their own hopes and dreams had fallen with him. For Orion's friends, it was a far more personal and grave spectacle taking place at the center of the grass, where brave Orion rose weakly, too battered and spent to fight but unwilling to submit.

Archidamus immediately moved in, unleashing a barrage of knees to the ribs that drove Orion to the ground again. There the Elean lay helpless on his back, much like Demosthenes had, minutes before. But Demosthenes was still in no condition to return the saving favor.

Now Aria, Cadmus, and Hipponax, sensing that Orion could be killed, desperately moved to a gap in the short wall at the front of the stands. They wanted to run into the competition area to stop the contest. But the Spartan ring placed their spears on Orion's friends to prevent them, and even gigantic Hipponax did not defy such force. Resisting would only result in death. So, powerless to help, they remained on their side of the wall and watched, hoping that Orion could somehow turn the tide.

On the arena floor, the Spartan king swaggered over to Orion and lifted him up from the grass. Then, raising Orion over his head, he slammed him down hard into the ground.

Orion landed on his back with a thud. And there he remained, unable to move but still conscious. With blurry vision and muffled hearing, he spotted Cadmus, restrained by Spartan weapons, calling to him. "Come on, Orion. Get up. You have to get up."

Blinking, Orion tried to focus as Aria came into view, standing next to Cadmus. Now Orion's thoughts flew back to the moment when she had given him the medallion, and a strange peace descended, even as the Spartan king went to one knee over him.

Archidamus, with his left hand, grabbed Orion by the hair, lifting Orion's head slightly off the ground, and then the Spartan raised his right hand, readying to deliver a finishing blow across his helpless opponent's neck.

Those in the terraces sat silent, waiting to witness the horrible sight of an athlete killed in competition. And even worse, soon they would be watching the death of an athlete who had won their hearts with his valor and compassion.

"Do you have any last words?" asked Archidamus, mocking Orion's attempt to redeem Nestor from his fate on the stake.

Orion tried to move his lips to answer. But he barely could. And no sound came out.

"What's that?" sarcastically elicited the gloating Spartan king, intending further insult, knowing that Orion wanted to speak but that he could not. "I can't hear you."

Strangely, Orion (with a weak but definite smile on his face) now responded by looking directly into his executioner's eyes. And then Archidamus followed Orion's eyes as the Elean moved them to focus on his own hand. It had previously rested limp on the ground under the Spartan, but now it was about to grasp him firmly by the testicles.

Archidamus' expression turned to horror just as Orion closed his grip and then suddenly increased the pressure to maximum, squeezing violently until the king, driven unconscious by pain, collapsed forward over him.

"Get up, Orion!" pleaded Hipponax, his desperation resonating through the bowl, heard by the entire stunned stadium crowd, hushed as it waited to see which of the two combatants could recover first to claim victory.

"*Orion, Orion, Orion!*" Cadmus began chanting, trying to rouse the crowd to use its power, and willingly it joined, vibrating with one voice, exhorting its hero. "*Orion, Orion, Orion!*"

The young Elean, finding his strength, pushed the still-unconscious Archidamus off and came to his feet. Aria crossed the wall and slipped by the stunned Spartan troops, who were all facing arena-center. She ran up to hug Orion. Tears streaming down her cheeks, she put her trembling lips to his.

Now the crowd cheered louder than ever.

Lycurgus seethed as he watched. In addition to allowing him to attack Athens by surprise, Lycurgus always had seen the games as the means to increase Spartan influence over the rest of Greece; as Olympic Champion, Archidamus would have projected the image of Spartan supremacy, thereby tempting the other cities to the Spartan side of the war. But now, Lycurgus had to come to terms with the fact that, despite everything, Orion had stolen that prize.

Swept up by the emotions of having just seen his best friend claim victory from the brink of oblivion, Cadmus grabbed a willing Medea and kissed her.

Orion, one arm around Aria, waved graciously with the other to the standing terrace crowd, which passionately invoked the young champion's name as if it would never stop. But then abruptly it did, changing to the sound of intense boos. Orion and Aria, realizing that the new chorus seemed to be directed behind, turned to see scowling Lycurgus, accompanied by five soldiers, including the Spartan captain, marching purposefully towards them across the grass. The older and more cunning king, skilled at hiding his true emotions, was too angered to exercise his usual control.

The stadium crowd, fearful of what Lycurgus would do, hushed as his party arrived at Orion and Aria. Suddenly, the Spartan captain whipped the Olympic Grand Champion's garland of olive leaves from behind his back and handed it to the monarch. Lycurgus then grudgingly placed it on Orion's bowed head.

Now the relieved stadium crowd, with one rhythmic voice, gave vent to its feelings, relentlessly alternating chants of Orion's name with double claps of hands.

The smiling Olympic Grand Champion from Elis, backing away from Lycurgus to wave at the spectators again, graciously accepted their praise. In the background, two soldiers helped Archidamus up, revived but even now quite pained.

But then Lycurgus, pride rising, Spartan and royal, brusquely pushed in front of Orion to angrily address the terrace crowd. "How dare you cheer this common sheepherder and in the same breath revile me? Have you forgotten that I represent true glory and power?"

The terraces responded with one long, low, resonating boo.

Even further enraged, Lycurgus shouted above the crowd. He never allowed anyone to challenge him without besting them. "While you fools exalt this meaningless victory, Sparta is winning a real victory far away."

Immediately sensing from Lycurgus' tone and demeanor that something was indeed terribly wrong, the stadium crowd fell silent.

"Yes," Lycurgus gloated, now that he had turned the tables to seize the upper hand. "I thought that would get your attention. I suppose now is as good a time as any to tell you that the great Spartan army was busy taking Athens while you all celebrated these foolish games."

"What about the truce?" Cleon challenged, though he was visibly shaken.

"Surely, you did not expect me to keep that ridiculous truce," chuckled Lycurgus. "Anyway, it is no longer of consequence. All that matters is that we presently hold Athens in our grip."

Then Lycurgus turned to his captain, commanding him firm and sure. "Seize this sheepherder, and take the Athenian delegation into custody."

Immediately, the Spartans attending Lycurgus pointed their spears and started towards Orion, who now pushed Aria behind himself, readying for combat. He would defend, even with his bare hands. And he would protect Aria at all costs.

But he would not have to do so alone. The dam had burst. Spartan corruption of the sacred festival had reached the point where Zeus himself would demand that those in the terrace crowd take a stand for him. And if they did not, then they risked divine retribution from the most feared of all gods, a prospect far worse than that which any Spartan weapon could inflict. Now the crowd would fight to save the Athenian delegation and the valiant

Olympic Champion, who had become a symbol of all that was right and true and good in the world. In so doing, the spectators would restore their own relationship with Zeus.

Suddenly, as one, inspired by Orion's bravery and resolve in overcoming Spartan injustice, every able-bodied man from the terrace crowd, regardless of affiliation and though unarmed, surged at the ring of Spartans, whom they far outnumbered, twenty to one.

"Kill them," shouted Archidamus, grabbing a sword from a soldier's sheath as he joined the ranks. "Kill them all."

Now the fearsome Spartans held the line strong, just behind the short wall that separated the terraces from the arena grass. Their spears and swords cleaved a good toll, cutting down many of the unarmed spectators closing around them in one enormous wave.

Orion, shielding Aria behind himself, disarmed his first assailant and claimed that soldier's spear to stave off Lycurgus and his four remaining men.

Despite their losses, those from the stadium crowd, coming with unfaltering determination, worked together to overcome some of the blood-red and shining bronze, taking the fallen soldiers' weapons to use against their Spartan comrades.

Soon the people of Greece fractured the Spartan line in various places and poured through the fissures, and now the battle spread across the arena floor as the soldiers broke their ranks to fight those who had gushed behind.

Hipponax and Cadmus, working together, recklessly fought their way through the sea of chaos on the Olympic grass. They were frantic to reach their friend in time to help him stave off the swarm of Spartans around Aria and him. Orion, using the stolen Spartan spear much like his trusted wooden staff, was for the moment (even as he kept Aria pressed close behind his back) holding his own against his assailants' greater number, through a variety of spectacular parries and thrusts.

Demosthenes and Archidamus, having stabbed past any enemy in the way, found one another, and they battled furiously, swords clashing hard as each slashed and blocked, intent on besting his hated nemesis.

Hipponax and Cadmus reached Orion, and the three Eleans, standing shoulder-to-shoulder, formed a triangle around Aria, each dealing rancor on any aggressor who advanced on his side.

Meanwhile, the whole tide turned for good. The united people of Greece, despite many painful sacrifices, through their resolve and their numbers, increasingly felled soldier after soldier to gain the upper hand. And within minutes, they finished the remaining Spartans, including the two kings.

Archidamus died at the point of Demosthenes' sword, stuck through the chest, right into his black heart, hate filling his eyes even as the last of his life spilled out onto the grass.

Lycurgus was pierced through the abdomen by Cadmus' blade, which came out his back a full foot. Unlike Archidamus, as Lycurgus sank to his knees, his eyes filled with regret, knowing that his own grave miscalculation was responsible for his ultimate demise. He never expected that the people from different cities would unite with each other in any meaningful way. The possibility certainly never entered his mind that they would come together, unarmed, to defeat nine hundred of his warriors, three times the number of fearsome Spartans that had held the whole Persian army for an entire week in the narrow mountain pass at Thermopylae, some sixty years previous.

Then Lycurgus' eyes turned blank, rolling back in his head as he slumped forward onto the ground, ended.

Chapter Sixteen

ALL HAIL

The battle over, those who were able removed the dead and tended the wounded. Cleon, among the gravely injured, was taken back to his luxurious room in the Ambassador Quarters. But even Hippocrates could not help, Cleon's spine having been severed just below chest level by a Spartan blade. Now the states-man lay in bed, each breath more labored than the last, as Demos-thenes and a host of mourners solemnly gathered around.

"Hold strong," urged the general, pretending a half-hearted smile.

"I am done for," panted Cleon, mouth dry as gravel. "Remind our people that Athens expects every man to do his duty—no matter what."

Then Cleon closed his eyes and gasped for the last time. Demosthenes waited a minute, looking to make sure his friend was final, and then he leaned over and kissed the great man on the cheek.

After dark, the crowd (composed of the remaining people from the six places besides the Amazon Island and Sparta) poured into the stadium terraces by the light of the three-day-old moon. Nine newly appointed men (two each from four cities and one from another) now replaced their fallen predecessors in the ten ambassador chairs, next to the lone remaining dignitary from Thebes. The ten Hellanodikes (having briskly fled through the stadium tunnel at the onset of the fighting earlier that day) returned intact to their seats on the opposite side of the stadium.

And all in the giant bowl were solemn as they watched the procession emerge single-file from the tunnel onto the stained arena grass. The twelve blonde-haired maidens in flowing white gowns came first. Orion, Demosthenes, Konon, Memnon, and Herak walked behind them—each holding a burning torch aloft in his right hand, the only man-made light in the entire bowl.

The procession arrived at arena-center and turned to face the Hellanodikes. Solorchus rose from the seat previously occupied by Lycurgus, walked towards Orion with a freshly cut olive garland in his hands, and placed it on the champion's bowed head to crown him properly. And still all was quiet, not a word spoken in the entire stadium, even as tears streamed down the young athlete's cheeks.

Solorchus retook his place at arena-side. Then one of the new ambassadors from Corinth rose to speak about the Hellanodikes. Together the people of all places, agreeing that the men in purple royal robes had not conducted themselves well, decided that their order, rather than consisting of men of entitlement, should be elected from among the people of Elis.

Next, Demosthenes spoke about the dishonor brought to the competition by the conduct of Memnon and Herak, and they were forbidden from ever again participating at the games. Then, Demosthenes directed his words to Athens' plight, asking the people of the other cities to align with it against the Spartans in the war outside. Elis was disgusted that the Spartans had forced shame on the games and readily allied with Athens. Argos and Mantinea, long enemies of their cruel neighbors to the south, also were eager to join. Thebes and Corinth refused solidarity with the new confederation of united cities, but they both agreed not to side with the Spartans against it.

The next morning, all ships sailed from the banks of the Alpheus away from Olympia. And those who had come by land began their trek home to prepare for imminent hostilities.

❧

Days later, word reached Marathon at his post behind Athens' Sacred Gateway that an armada of ships was coming to port, Demosthenes' own vessel among them. Immediately, the young captain, riding a horse and trailing another, stormed to Piraeus. He met Demosthenes as the general disembarked. And Marathon recounted the latest events while the two galloped between the long walls, into the city, past the Acropolis, through the Agora, and towards the Dipylon Gateway.

As Demosthenes rode towards Athens' main entrance, he was taken aback by the effectiveness of the destruction rendered by the Spartans' new weapon. The previously unbreakable city wall, manned atop the ramparts and behind, through repeated battering, was breached in several places near the ground. And the enemy could flow through these gaps without having to cross the courtyards of either the Dipylon or Sacred Gateways.

General Nicias stood atop the Dipylon's left front tower looking out at the assembled Spartan army; its ten catapults at the back of the troops, Brasidas stood in front of his full force, preparing them for a massive infantry assault. Now that the Athenian defenses had been softened and Athenian morale broken, the Spartan general was fully confident that his men could at least enter the city. And they might even take it.

But that confidence was shaken right out, just as Brasidas was about to give the order to go forward. A rider (blood-red cape flying in the wind, sounding a horn to gather attention) charged down from the coastal range behind the Spartan camp and raced through to the front of the formation. Reliable word of their comrades' demise at the games had reached Sparta. And this rider had been sent to summon the troops immediately back to defend the homeland, in the event that it should be attacked by the powerful new alliance against it.

Now, instead of marching his army into battle, Brasidas sent the lone rider to the walls of Athens with a message for its leaders to meet him in the ground between their two armies to discuss terms of peace.

An hour later, Brasidas came alone to meet the three elected to speak for Athens—Demosthenes, Nicias, and glamorous Colonel Alcibiades, Pericles' arrogant nephew who had enjoyed ridiculing Orion when he first appeared before Athens' council to proclaim the games.

There, in the open ground between the two armies, Brasidas proposed a peace of fifty years between Sparta and Athens, each to conduct its own way of life and foreign affairs free of interference from the other.

"The terms sound reasonable," replied Nicias, recognizing that Pericles himself would have liked the outcome.

"Then, you accept?" urged Brasidas.

"Not yet," Nicias replied. "In Athens, it is not up to a few men. Our elected council must decide."

"You have one hour," snapped Brasidas, irritated.

The three from Athens turned and walked back towards the Dipylon Gateway, discussing as they went. After all that Demosthenes had been through in trying to secure lasting peace, he firmly believed that the Spartans did not really want it and that Brasidas was just trying to defuse their immediate disadvantage. Athens must press its present position of numbers and alliances to decimate the reeling Spartans. If it didn't, in a few years, the new confederation of united cities might dissipate, and then the regrouped Spartans could surge again, perhaps stronger than before. But Nicias, chief of all generals, wanted to accept the peace, especially when Alcibiades backed him, though Nicias was too simple to see why the younger man did.

Twenty minutes later, the entire five hundred members of the Athenian Council convened in the rectangular hall with the green-marble debate floor, five rows of long benches on both sides, and walls painted with life-sized scenes of gods and heroes. Nicias spoke first. Next, Demosthenes stated his position. And then Alcibiades rose from his seat in the gallery. Cunning and ambition winning out over Athens' well-being, he supported Nicias and overstated the case against Demosthenes as maker of war and nothing else, even though in his heart he knew that the man he slandered was in fact both certainly righteous and quite possibly right. Long had Alcibiades looked for the opportunity to rise to prominence, waiting in the wings while men like Demosthenes, older and more established, were still in their prime as men of influence and able to swat away his challenge. But now, by backing Nicias—something he might naturally do without being accused of convenience since Pericles was mentor to both Nicias and him—Alcibiades could move Demosthenes to the side. Then Alcibiades—as the architect of the general's final fall from grace—could ascend in Demosthenes' place.

Demosthenes was little surprised at Alcibiades. The general had long been wary of the fast-rising upstart, realizing that Alcibiades inordinately craved power and fame for their own sake and not for use in service of the people who bestowed it. But Demosthenes was surprised at how quickly the council, except Socrates and Captain Marathon, turned on him and branded him an extremist.

Yet, mindful of Cleon's last words, Demosthenes swallowed his pride and argued for Athens' sake, despite a growing sense that it would cost him personally. "You are all so hungry for a life without war that you eagerly accept an illusion of calm. But I warn you, it will be only temporary, and Athens will eventually suffer a terrible fate if we do not fight now to win a real peace that will endure!"

The council responded by removing Demosthenes from the ranks of leadership, demoting him to captain. The insult hurt the now former general, but it did not sting nearly as much as when the council voted to accept Sparta's proposal.

That same day, as the sun set, the 292 Spartan prisoners—taken four years ago by Demosthenes at the Island of Wasps—walked out of the Dipylon Gateway towards their cheering brothers. The next morning, the entire invading army was gone, much to most everyone's relief.

Orion, Cadmus, and Hipponax had come to Athens with the armada, intent on helping protect the city. Urged by the remaining Plataeans, Demosthenes had given the Eleans the dull-black iron tools of war that had belonged to three of the mustard scorpions' fallen brothers. And the general had stationed the Eleans with him and the Plataeans, halfway between the Dipylon Gateway and the Agora's mouth, on the broad road that led towards the Acropolis. Demosthenes and his men were to have been the last barrier between the Spartans and the innocents—including Aria and Medea—sheltered among its magnificent white-marble buildings. But the fight never came. And when the enemy suddenly withdrew, the Eleans happily set down their weapons and their armor.

A month later, Orion and Cadmus, watched by thousands atop the ramparts, stood inside the Dipylon Courtyard hugging Hipponax. Then the giant mounted a massive rust-red stallion and galloped away from Athens, on his way home to Elis. There he would take up life with his wife at his two friends' now former residence.

The next day, Orion moved to the farm outside Athens (complete with olive groves and sheep) that the people of the city had gifted to honor the Olympic Champion. Aria joined him there as his bride. Medea went to live with Cadmus on the farm next door, bought by Pytheas for his younger daughter and her new husband.

Though happy for them, Pytheas missed his children. But each Sunday for the next year, his pain was relieved as they returned with their men to the blue-walled andron of his house. There they feasted, always loud and never quiet.

And for everyone else in Athens, too, the best of times were here again. The city, having restored life without war, flourished once more to grandeur reminiscent of its Golden Age, and its people were often heard shouting.

"All hail the Peace of Nicias!"

"All hail the Peace of Nicias!"

"All hail the Peace of Nicias!"

The Adventure Continues...

MANTINEA 418
The Lust For War

ACKNOWLEDGEMENTS

We would like to thank the following people:

Harry and Brenda Bissoon-Dath, Phyllis and Brian Barrette, Mackenna, Max, Drew, Pat LoBrutto, Ken Doo of Ken Doo Photography, Mark Deamer, Jeanne Pietrzak of Graphic Gold, Penny Callmeyer, Don and Heather Cox, Alex Tomaich, Alex Aliferis, Dan Wikstrom of DarkHeart Armoury, James Jones, Le Chi Truong, Kevin Spillane, Mel and Rawle Lewis, Julie Burns, Adalberto Garcia, Rebecca Plude, Jean Thompson, Getachew Sequar, Vi Tran, Patrick Mayer and Michele Johnson (and everyone else at Common Grounds), Aaron Peterson, Julia Beckhusen, Shannon McHenry, J.D. and Chris Denton, Skeeter and Roger Resler, Hagi Ariel, and Spencer Kenner.